Defender
Of The Faith

Defender
Of The Faith
Charles Ludwig

BETHANY HOUSE PUBLISHERS
MINNEAPOLIS, MINNESOTA 55438
A Division of Bethany Fellowship, Inc.

Published by Bethany House Publishers
A Division of Bethany Fellowship, Inc.
6820 Auto Club Road, Minneapolis, Minnesota 55438

Printed in the United States of America

Library of Congress Cataloging-in-Publication Data

Ludwig, Charles, 1918–
   Defender of the faith / Charles Ludwig.
      p.   cm.

    1. Victoria, Queen of Great Britain, 1819–1901—Fiction.
I. Title.
PS3523.U434D44   1988
813'.52—dc19   88–22116
ISBN 1-87123-999-X   CIP

In memory of my father J. S. Ludwig,
distinguished missionary to Kenya.
Like Queen Victoria, he was convinced
that the most powerful weapons
are spiritual.

About the Author

Author Charles Ludwig grew up on the mission field in Kenya. He brings to his historical novels with BHP an impressive writing experience, having more than forty books already published, several of which have been read or dramatized on worldwide radio. Ludwig also has a rich pastoral and evangelistic ministry, having preached across Europe and in many other countries. He and his wife make their home in Tucson, Arizona. Biographical novels with BHP include:

Queen of the Reformation—Katie Luther
Mother of an Army—Catherine Booth
Champion of Freedom—Harriet Beecher Stowe
Defender of the Faith—Queen Victoria

Foreword

Since truth is more exciting—and more incredible—than responsible fiction, readers may ask, "How much of this story is true?" The answer is, *All of it is true*. Victoria, *Defender of the Faith*, and *Providential Queen*, was guided by the Lord.

True, we have put words in her mouth, and in the mouths of others. Likewise, we've invented a few very minor scenes, but we've only done so when the words or scenes were extremely probable.

Queen Victoria kept an extensive journal. She often wrote ten pages a day. In addition, she was a prolific letter writer. Parts of her journal and letters have been used by many, and we have dipped into numerous books where her letters and journal have been reproduced. We have given credit for most of these quotations, but it would be impossible to be completely accurate, for it would be difficult to name the writer who first used the paragraph from her journal or one of her letters.

My only invented name is Pegasus—a name I conferred on her favorite stallion.

Preface

Every year Canada, along with other British Common-wealth Nations, celebrates Empire Day. This gala event honors Queen Victoria who was born on May 24, 1819—the year Alabama entered the Union.

Celebrations begin on the 23rd and continue through the 24th. During the first day, schools have special programs, and on the following day there are colorful parades. Empire Day is not a religious holiday. Nonetheless, it provides opportunity for the churches to emphasize the providence of God. And this they do with enthusiasm, for regardless of the way Queen Victoria is viewed, all must admit that incredible providence was the major ingredient which placed her on the British throne and kept her there for more than sixty-three glorious years.

That Victoria became Queen at the age of eighteen was indeed a miracle. This is so for many reasons, two of which are quite startling. The first is that Victoria had only a few drops of British blood. Her father was of German descent. Her mother was German. Her governess was German. And even though she was born in London's Kensington Palace, she was conceived on the Continent. Moreover, her baby talk was German. This was because her parents, when alone, conversed in German.

Alexandrina Victoria—her full name—did not begin to learn English until she was three. But being German was not fatal. Both ancestors, George I and George II, were German, and George I never even attempted to learn English.

Victoria's second startling obstacle in becoming Queen of Great Britain was family competition. George the III had fathered fifteen legitimate heirs, in addition to the offspring he had by Hannah Lightfoot. Of these, five princesses and seven princes—the Prince of Wales and six dukes—had survived. Had these twelve been as prolific as their parents, they would have produced 180 children. Also, since each of George's children would have been heirs, there would have been 192 individuals with royal blood and a chance to reign. Indeed, two of them became kings.

Yet in spite of these problems, Victoria was crowned Queen of the British Empire on June 28, 1838.

Victoria's reign was not only the longest in British history, it was also the most sublime. During her years on the throne, Britain experienced vast industrial growth, a great increase and consolidation of empire, and, most important of all, a vital missionary trust. Among the host of great missionaries in her time were David Livingstone, Alexander Mackay, Mary Slessor, James Hudson Taylor, and Bishop James Hannington.

When their lives were imperiled, these giants found it almost as advantageous to mention they were subjects of the "Queenie" as Paul did when he reminded his captors that he was a Roman citizen. Believing in fairness, possessing the world's largest navy, and living a chaste Christian life, Queen Victoria was respected around the world.

The word *providence* was an oft repeated word at the beginning of the nineteenth century. This is because of providential deliverances from storms, wars, plagues, and especially Napoleon Bonaparte.

Providence placed Victoria on the throne, kept her there, and altered the events of the next sixty-three years in a most positive way.

Table of Contents

1
The Royal Birth

Bone-weary, the Archbishop of Canterbury continued to pace back and forth in the breakfast room of Kensington Palace. At Lambeth Palace, documents requiring immediate attention piled high on his desk. Yet he was unable to leave. A potential king or queen was on the verge of being born in a room adjacent to where he paced. The law insisted that he be on hand to ascertain the genuineness of the forthcoming prince or princess.

The Archbishop bit his lip and glanced at the grandfather clock. He did not relish this task. But history forced him to remain with the Cabinet ministers who had been assigned to verify the birth. A quarrel over the baby could lead to bloodshed.

For two years, an urgent race to deliver an heir consumed the House of Hanover. This baby, waiting to be born, might be the fulfillment of that race.

At 3:50 A.M., a frantic knock on the breakfast room door startled him. "My lord," half-shouted a servant. "You are needed in the birthing room. Immediately!"

The Archbishop joined the others: the Bishop of London, the Duke of Wellington, the Chancellor of the Exchequer, Lord Bathurst, Lord Lanadowne, and the Duke of Sussex.

Precisely at 4 A.M, a lusty cry filled the room. "It's a girl," announced the doctor.

The Duke of Kent leaned over his wife. "I told you it would be a girl," he exulted after he had kissed the new mother. "And she's a beauty. She's as fat as a partridge."

The nearly chinless baby snuggled up to Victoire for breakfast. Her mother happily obliged.

A voice broke the contented sounds of nursing. "Excuse me, madam. We'll get you a wet nurse."

The Duchess of Kent smiled. "You can get one later. But right now she's hungry."

The tall figure blushed. "As you wish, madam," he said as he bowed out of the room.

The round baby, knowing only what she wanted, continued to feed until satisfied. Her tummy full, she drifted off to sleep.

The Duke of Kent, excited by his daughter's vitality, wrote to the Duke of Orleans, "The little one is rather a pocket of Hercules than a pocket of Venus." He gloated to special friends, in an anything-but-confidential tone, that her destiny was to become a famous queen.

The Duchess of Kent snuggled her baby, smelling the newness of life. Her joy mingled with sadness as her mind replayed the events of England's past two years. The events began with the tragedy of Princess Charlotte who never had the joy of snuggling her child.

King George III, old, ill and insane, no longer exercised ruling power for the kingdom. Thus, his eldest son, George Augustus Frederick, was appointed Regent. The saddened country found joy in the pregnancy of Princess Charlotte, the only child of the Regent. She was not only the heir presumptive, but everyone loved her.

As she went into labor, the whole country focused on their beloved Princess. Her labor dragged on for forty-eight hours.

When her labor ended, the Archbishop of Canterbury entered the birthing room. The obstetrician looked at the Archbishop and shook his head. "It was a boy," he announced sadly. "But I'm afraid, my lord, that he was stillborn."

Another doctor added, "We did all we could to bring him to life. We slapped him, dipped him in cold water and then hot water. We rubbed him with salt, covered him with mustard and manipulated his chest."

The doctor noticed the Archbishop viewing the well-formed baby. His voice took on a note of despair. "My lord, it was to no avail. His mother was in labor far too long. Perhaps we should have used forceps. He didn't take a single breath. Not one."

The Archbishop looked away from the baby to Charlotte's anguished husband. "Prince Leopold, your whole life is before you. Her Royal Highness is only twenty-one. The Lord may still bless you with many children."

In spite of her many hours in labor, Princess Charlotte sat up in bed and lunched on toast and chicken broth. Confident that she was doing well, all the witnesses, including the Prince, excused themselves to return to their homes to rest.

One of the Archbishop's servants awakened him from a deep sleep. "My lord," he said excitedly, "a messenger has just come from Claremont House to see you. He said it's very important."

"And what is it?"

"He said that you should be prepared to return with him to the birthing room in Claremont House."

The Archbishop splashed cold water on his face and dressed. He strode outside and into the carriage. "What's the problem?" he inquired of the doctor in the front seat.

"Her Royal Highness, Princess Charlotte, passed away at two-thirty this morning."

The Archbishop stared. "But—but she was well when I left!"

"True. We were all confident that she would recover. She seemed fine until a little after midnight. Then she began to complain of nausea and ringing in her ears."

"What did you do to help her?" he demanded.

"We gave her hot wine and brandy and placed hot water bottles and warm flannel on her abdomen. But all that did was to make her complain that she was getting tipsy. She continued to hemorrhage. We . . ."

"I thought *cold* water was used to stop hemorrhaging," interrupted the Archbishop.

"It usually is," agreed the doctor. "But, my lord, Sir Richard was in charge. He ordered the hot wine and brandy and hot water bottles. For a time, I thought she'd pull through. Then she began to have spasms. My lord, we were helpless."[1]

The Archbishop shook his head. "She would have been a great queen. I do hope her death doesn't cause a scandal. A scandal right now could be extremely damaging." He sighed. "The good Lord knows we need a few years of peace and quiet." He shook his head and turned up his collar against the draft that seeped into the coach.

After a long silence, the doctor said, "I heard you were at Windsor. How is His Majesty doing?"

"His mind is completely gone. The only thing he seems to remember is that he is George III. His beard is snow-white and reaches halfway down his chest. He is also totally blind." The Archbishop sighed. "While I tried to visit with him, he paced around in his violet dressing gown. He didn't know me."

The doctor frowned. "Francis Willis was the first doctor assigned to him. His idea was that the will of the King should be broken in the same way in which a wild horse is broken. In order to break his spirit, they tied and gagged him. The assistants, together with the Prince of Wales and the Duke of York were encouraged to mock him."

"That would be enough to make me insane," the Archbishop commented. "Didn't they also apply leeches?"

"Oh yes, plenty of them. Subsequent doctors blistered his feet with Spanish Fly and mustard plasters."

"Spanish Fly and mustard plasters? What are those for?" the Archbishop asked.

---

[1] Today, medical scientists believe she died of a pulmonary embolism.

"The Spanish Fly is made from green blister beetles. They, together with the mustard plaster are supposed to draw out his rebellious tendencies."

The Archbishop nodded. "I would think his wicked, utterly corrupt sons have been the final blow to his already fragile mind."

"No doubt. I dread the day when His Majesty dies and the Regent is crowned George IV."

In the ornate living room lit with candles, the Archbishop faced both the Regent and the Prince. "I've come to offer my condolences," he said. "The entire country is saddened. But we must remember that our Heavenly Father is sovereign. He does not make mistakes. In addition, I want you to know that I am certain that both Princess Charlotte and her son are now with the Lord. Let me read to you from the Holy Scriptures."

Later that night, as the Archbishop prepared for bed, his mind sorted out the apparent inevitable events of the immediate future.

George III would soon pass away. That fact no one would deny. Then the brandy-soaked Regent would succeed him as George IV. And he, the Archbishop of Canterbury, would be forced to crown him at his coronation. Horrors! Being subject to such a sot would be dreadful.

As he slipped into his nightclothes, he shuddered at his coming responsibility of having to crown the tall, multicorseted, heavily rouged man. A larger horror soon took over his thoughts. The Regent's estranged wife, Caroline of Brunswick, no doubt would return to England and demand to be crowned Queen.

During the years the Regent had been the Prince of Wales, he had married Maria Fitzherbert. He loved her deeply. But no royal marriage was legal without the King's consent. George III insisted that his eldest son leave Maria and marry Caroline of Brunswick.

George Augustus Frederick neither wanted to leave Maria nor marry Caroline. When his father insisted, he countered with a bargain. "I'll marry her if Parliament pays my debts," he promised. Parliament complied even though it set the treasury back one hundred and ten thousand pounds.

The unhappy couple were united on April 8, 1796.

They separated after a year of misery in which Caroline had given birth to Charlotte. Caroline accused him of drinking too much and being too fat. He accused her of drinking too much and of smelling bad.

Caroline fled to Italy. Forgetting her husband was the Prince of Wales, she paraded in flesh-colored tights, had an affair with a gigolo and often appeared at distinguished parties seminude.

The Archbishop sat heavily on his bed. Heartsick, the leader of the Church of England prayed for guidance.

The entire United Kingdom reeled from the shock of their beloved Charlotte's death and the death of her son, their future king. Three months following the funeral, after being unmercifully blamed for both the deaths of Charlotte and her son, Sir Richard Croft committed suicide.

During the aftermath of public hysteria, talk flowed freely about the future of the country.

It seemed to all observers that if the country was to have a second generation heir, that heir would have to be fathered by one of three men: the Duke of Kent, the Duke of Clarence or the Duke of Cambridge.

The three eligible bachelors who were being pressured to produce a second-generation heir took the challenge seriously. Each believed it would be a high honor to be remembered in history as the father of a king or queen.

In addition to this honor, Edward, the Duke of Kent, along with William, the Duke of Clarence had an additional incentive. Overwhelmed by debt, the increased income from Parliament for supporting an heir would keep at least some of their more vicious creditors at bay.

Edward had already been looking for a princess to mother a legal heir for more than two years. Even before Charlotte's death, he had been disappointed in his search until a friend directed his attention to Princess Victoire of Saxe-Coburg. "True," the friend explained, "she's a widow and has two children. But she's just a little over thirty and is a sister of Prince Leopold, the husband of your niece, Princess Charlotte. Her blood is as royal as it is possible for royal blood to be."

Edward's eyes widened. "Go on."

"After Napoleon divorced Josephine for not giving him an heir, Victoire was on his list of suitable princesses. She was then only sixteen. Maybe that's why he married someone else."

"Sound's interesting. But where is Saxe-Coburg?" Edward frowned.

"It's in the heart of Germany at the base of the Thuringian mountains. It's a tiny, tiny place. Less than fifty thousand people live there. Still, it's famous. If you know the history of Doctor Martin Luther, you know about his experience in the Fortress of Coburg."

"You mean where he hid from Emperor Charles V, translating the Old Testament?"

"Precisely."

Edward walked around the room, stroking his chin. "Now tell me about Victoire. What kind of roots does she have?"

"She's from the House of Saxe-Coburg, a branch from the House of Wettin. The Wettins have been rulers since the eleventh century."

"What about her former husband?"

"As the Prince of Leiningen-Dachsburg-Hadenburgh, instead of making plans for his country, the old boy wasted his time hunting and drinking. When he died in 1814, Victoire became Regent. She's a good one. Her handful of subjects have prospered."

"Do you know anything *bad* about her?" Edward slanted his eyes.

"Not really. She is a little plump."

They both laughed.

Convinced that Victoire was just the princess he needed, Edward borrowed enough money for the trip and went to see her. Knowing that time was of the essence, for his brothers were already combing the lists of princesses, he planned his approach as carefully as a diamond cutter plans his strategy with an unusually fine diamond. Viewing himself in the mirror, he realized that he was not as handsome as many. He was fat, half-bald, and fierce-looking. He attempted to repair his looks by dying his hair black and sporting wide sideburns that nearly curved to his lips.

In addition to touching up his face, Edward prepared for his first meeting with Victoire by donning a splendid field marshal's uniform. The heavy gold braid on the high collar was especially impressive, as were his various medals. Also, he had fortified himself with a letter of introduction from Princess Charlotte.

Both Victoire and her two children impressed Edward. Prince Charles and Princess Feodora were extremely polite and responded to him with curious respect and courtesy.

Not wasting a second, Edward handed Victoire the letter from her sister-in-law, and even before she had time to read it, made his proposal. Victoire couldn't hide her shock. "I-I-I'll h-h-have to think about it," she replied.

Although Edward had to leave Amorbach without a definite commitment, he could not forget her soft brown eyes and slender face framed in dark curls. Memories of her spiced his dreams. He became determined that she would be his wife and mother of his children. But as he considered the situation, he realized he had asked her to make a great sacrifice. As Regent, she received five thousand pounds a year, had a comfortable home and had subjects who adored her. If she married him, she must move to England, learn English and give up her regency.

Knowing he needed help to bring an affirmation from a lady who had already been burned by one marriage, Edward asked both Leopold and Charlotte to correspond with her and explain to her the advantages of marrying him. He also kept a stream of letters flowing to her written in French.

In spite of his most ardent pleas, the brown-eyed princess continued to hesitate. Finally, when Charlotte lost her baby and died, he realized he could no longer procrastinate. His letters continued to plead. Victoire continued to hesitate.

Early in January, 1818, Edward's patience reached its limit. Selecting a fresh quill and a sheaf of blank paper, he wrote the most ardent letter of his career. He explained that he was quite willing for her to vacation for several months in Germany each year, that even though she lost her regency she would become the Duchess of Kent and receive an income from Parliament. He also emphasized that she might become the mother of a king or queen of the world's largest empire. He closed by demanding an immediate yes or no answer.

Her resistance worn down, Victoire finally accepted Edward's proposal. He received her reply on January 25. They eagerly made plans for their public betrothal. They decided it would take place in Germany on May 28 and their formal wedding would be the next day.

The happy couple exchanged rings on the 28th. The next day they stood before the Lutheran minister. The Duke, resplendent in his field marshal's uniform, smiled at Victoire who stood vivaciously in an elaborate bridal gown.

At the end of the ceremony, the fortress guns boomed a salute. As they fired, the Duchess squeezed the Duke's hand, "I do love a gun salute," she whispered.

That evening, while the guests filed into an elaborate state dinner, the bride and groom were ceremoniously escorted to their apartment.

The feasting lasted until early morning.

Five days later, the Duke and Duchess headed for England and their British ceremony according to the rites of the Church of England.

By this time, the Duke of Clarence also had a bride-to-be; Adelaide of Saxe-Meiningen. Thus it was decided to have a double ceremony. The couples exchanged vows in the drawing-room at Kew. The Regent gave away both brides as the Archbishop of Canterbury and the Bishop of London officiated.

The Duke of Cambridge married Princess Augusta of Hesse-Cassel. Thus all three of the royal bachelors married within ten months after the death of Princess Charlotte.

Parliament cheered. A new heir would soon be forthcoming. No one thought about the mistresses the dukes were forsaking.

2
The Race for the Throne

By the middle of November, all three princesses announced to their delighted husbands that they were expecting a baby. According to their calculations, these heirs would be born in the early or late spring of 1819.

The United Kingdom was ecstatic. *Yes, the expected heirs would make the Hanoverian line safe!* A number of publications featured a cartoon which showed the dukes standing behind their seated wives, each of whom had an enormous abdomen.

Right after their marriage, the Duke and Duchess of Kent returned to Victoire's former kingdom to live. Now, as the snows in Amorbach began to melt, Edward took Victoire into his arms. "I think our little heir should be born in England," he announced.

Victoire looked troubled. "Why?"

"Because I have a feeling our baby will be a girl and that she will eventually become the queen."

Victoire's troubled eyes brightened. "A girl?" she demanded, lifting her voice. "Why do you think it will be a girl?"

"Because a gypsy fortune-teller told me I was to become the father of a great queen."

Victoire laughed. "Surely you don't believe in fortune-tellers! The Bible is against them."

"Well, maybe. Still—" He shrugged. "I shall write to the Regent today and ask him to make arrangements for us to stay in Kensington Palace until she's born."

"Will he agree?"

"Probably not. George would like to have his own heir. But since he's been separated from Caroline for twenty years, that's impossible. I think he's a little jealous. I'll be diplomatic and write to him in care of his private secretary, Sir Benjamin Bloomfield. Sir Benjamin is a good old boy and will soften him up. At least I hope he will."

Edward listed his requests for his wife:

1. For money to make the trip to Calais.
2. The use of the Royal yacht.
3. The loan of apartments in Kensington Palace.
4. Arrangements for us to eat.
5. Should her doctor so order, use of one of the houses at Brighton so that she can go sea bathing after the birth.

"You forgot one thing," complained Victoire.

"Yes?" He lifted his brows.

"You forgot to demand a gun salute when we land."

Edward frowned. "Are you serious?"

"Of course I'm serious. We both have royal blood. And, we are going to be the parents of a royal heir."

They both laughed. Then Victoire stood up. "Do you think your brother will grant your requests?"

"I doubt it. But if he doesn't, I'll find another way. Our child *will* be born in London!"

While the Duke and Duchess anxiously awaited a letter from the Regent, her morning sickness continued. "I do hope I don't have a miscarriage," she groaned after losing her breakfast.

December gave way to January. Still no reply. "George has always been stubborn," grumbled Edward as he paced the floor. "He was that way as a boy. Father used to beat him. It did no good." He rubbed his sideburns. "Pig-headed stubbornness is one of our family's least desirable characteristics."

One snowy morning, a special messenger handed a thick envelope to the Duke. As Edward read and reread the official document, his face whitened. Then he put his arms around Victoire. "The reply is just what I thought it would be."

"What did he say?"

"He said we should be willing to have our baby right here. Both the Duchess of Clarence and the Duchess of Cambridge are preparing to have their babies in Hanover."

"What are you going to do?"

"I'll borrow the money and we'll go on our own." He got up, walked to the window and glowered at the mountains.

Victoire clasped her hands together in her lap. "If we do that, will they let us cross the channel in the royal yacht and give us a gun salute?"

"Yes, I'll force them to do just that."

"How?"

"Simple. I'll tell the Regent that if he doesn't supply the Royal yacht we'll cross on the *Packet*."

Victoire shuddered. "The *Packet* is very rough. A friend crossed on it. She said it rolled and tossed like a cork. I might miscarry."

"That's the point. You have precious cargo within you. If you lost it on a rough voyage, the Regent would be blamed. The papers would hound him to death." Edward grinned. "I have that eldest brother of mine by the nose and I'm not going to let go regardless of how loud he squeals."

Victoire laughed. "I'm convinced that there is a stubborn streak in the House of Hanover!" She got up and kissed him on the cheek.

As the Duke's caravan prepared to leave for Calais on March 28, he shuddered at the unnecessary luggage his wife insisted on taking. Viewing each vehicle, he shook his head. "Do we *really* need all of this?" he demanded, sweeping his hand at the stacks of things.

"Of course. Didn't you say that I'm carrying precious cargo? I need to be safe." The Duchess spoke without blinking.

"But our bed? Why do you take our bed? We have any number of beds in England."

"True, but I'm accustomed to *this* bed."

"And do you really need Madame Siebold?" He made a face.

"Certainly. She's an obstetrician."

"But there are English doctors."

"Madame Siebold is both a qualified doctor and surgeon. She's a graduate of the University of Gottingen."

The Duke laughed. "The blood of the Wettins is just as stubborn as the blood of the Hanoverians. And now, even while we speak, that blood is mixing together in the poor little heir we're producing. The good Lord will have to extend mercy!"

They both laughed.

Edward arranged for the Duchess to ride in a cane-built phaeton. This light carriage had adequate springs and was more comfortable than the heavy-wheeled, nearly springless carriages which followed.

According to the carefully made plans, the caravan would travel twenty-five miles each day, then spend the night in an adequate inn. They rested for an entire day after each three days of travel.

At one stop, a French newspaper attracted Victoire. "Look at this," she exclaimed, "the Duchess of Cambridge gave birth to a healthy son on March 26. On the next day, Adelaide, the Duchess of Clarence had a daughter. But her daughter only lived seven hours."

"That's too bad," murmured Edward after he set down his cup of coffee.

"Where does that place our baby in the lineup of heirs?" asked Victoire eagerly.

"Let's see," replied the Duke. He took a short pencil from his pocket and began to draw a chart. "It's like this." He numbered each person in their legal order.

1. The Regent will become George IV when father dies.
2. Next in line is Frederick, the Duke of York.

3. Then comes William, the Duke of Clarence.
4. Following him is myself, the Duke of Kent.
5. Then, after my death, would be our firstborn."

Victoire nodded, thinking out loud. "Our child will be number five."

Edward put his hand on her arm. "However, you must remember that if my three older brothers have children, their children would be ahead of ours."

She leaned forward. "How possible is that?"

The Duke leaned back in his chair. He stroked his sideburns with a studied thoughtfulness. "The Regent, of course, will not have any children unless he divorces Caroline. He's not about to do that."

"How about Frederick, the Duke of York?"

"Fred has been legally married since 1791. So far, he and his Duchess have not even had the hint of a baby. So I don't think they'll ever have one. The one who *may* have a family is William, the Duke of Clarence. Since Adelaide had one child, it's probable she'll have another. If she does, that heir will be ahead of ours."

Following a little more than three weeks of difficult travel, the caravan limped into Calais on April 18. To the relief of everyone, the Royal yacht gently tossed in the harbor.

After a few days rest, the yacht began its historic journey. The fairly smooth sea allowed them to cross in less than four hours. Victoire became very ill with seasickness, spending most of the crossing bent over a basin.

While the captain skillfully guided the yacht into the harbor, a battery of guns began to fire a salute. Immensely pleased, the Duchess left her basin to wave at the crowds assembled on the wharf.

When the caravan reassembled, the Duke climbed to his seat on the phaeton and encouraged the horses into action. The trip across the Kentish countryside entailed two days of hard travel.

Each time they passed through a town or village, lines of people came to cheer and doff their hats.

At the end of the second day, as the sun painted the western horizon crimson, the Duke guided the phaeton into the parking strip of Kensington Palace.

Due to a mix-up over money, the repairs on their apartment had not been completed when they arrived. As they toured the rooms, the Duchess turned to her husband, her hands on her hips. "The apartment will have to be better than this," she complained.

"Never mind," assured the Duke. "I'll see to it that it's just about perfect."

Within days the apartment, which had not been occupied for five years, began to glisten with signs of prosperity. The rooms included a suite of large reception rooms, a nursery equipped with a mahogany bed and a matching crib. Each room had more than adequate closets. Red curtains and carpets graced the dining room. The living room had mirrors on the walls, historic paintings, a desk, bookshelves and a dozen "stool back" chairs.

From the tall windows, the Duchess could look out upon finely molded lawns, hedges formed into the shapes of birds, castles and animals. Wide-limbed beech and chestnut trees cast intriguing shadows. Many of these trees supported nests of sweet-singing birds.

The Duke spent several thousand pounds of borrowed money on the best furniture possible, and made certain that furniture had been properly arranged in the rooms. As Edward and Victoire surveyed the rooms, he put his arm around the Duchess. "Well, my dear, how do you like it?" he asked her.

"It's fit for a king," she sighed, kissing him on the cheek.

"It's also fit for a queen," he added with a laugh.

At about 10 P.M. on Sunday night, May 23, the Duchess stirred in her bed. "I think my time has come," she said. Her few words caused many to spring into action.

Victoire chased away thoughts of the past and snuggled her baby closer, ignoring the murmured talk around her.

Everyone, with the exception of the Regent, was happy with the yet unnamed infant. Having lost both his only legal child and his grandson, he was bitterly disappointed that he was not the father of a first-in-line heir. Moreover, his intense bitterness was made even more acute by his physical condition. Gout, overweight, and painful legs kept him in constant misery. This misery was intensified by his addiction to overdosing himself with opium.

In spite of the Regent's poorly suppressed hostility, the Duke and Duchess of Kent persuaded him to become a godfather at the forthcoming christening ceremonies.

Edward and Victoire spent many happy hours planning the baptism and naming of their little heir. In addition to the Regent, they decided the other godfather would be the Emperor of Russia, Alexander I. The godmothers would be the Duke of Kent's oldest sister, the Queen of Wurttemberg, and the mother of Victoire, the Dowager Duchess of Coberg.

The Duke and Duchess decided the child's name should be Victoire Georgiana Alexandrina Charlotte Augusta.

The Regent announced the date for the baptism as Monday, June 24 at 3 P.M. He also sent word to the Duke and Duchess that the occasion was to be private. He then listed the names of those to be invited. Also, he stated, there was to be no dressing up, no gold braid or uniforms. He would only allow simple garments such as frocks and normal dress suits.

Victoire felt heartsick. "It is obvious he dislikes us," she said as she wiped her eyes.

On the Sunday evening before the christening, the Regent rushed a note to the Duke and Duchess. Written in the third person, his message expressed his dislike of the names chosen for their baby and the sequence in which they appeared. He insisted the name Georgiana was not to be used "as he did not chuse (sic) to place the name before the Emperor of Russia and he would not allow it to follow." He also forbad the names Augusta and Charlotte. As to the final name, he indicated it would be decided in the midst of the ceremony.

The Cupola Room at Kensington Palace was prepared for

the ceremony. Crimson draperies made of velvet and borrowed from the Royal Chapel at St. James hung on the walls. The "gold" font for the baptism was brought from the Tower of London.

The private service began at 3 P.M. The tense situation became more tense as the minutes passed. The Regent was obviously unhappy. He refused to speak to the Duke of Kent.

At the proper time, the Archbishop of Canterbury took the child in his arms. As he prepared to dip his hand in the water, he turned to the Regent. "By what name shall I baptize this child?"

"Alexandria," barked the freshly rouged Regent. He spoke quickly, in a manner indicating he had considered the name for a long time.

"Add another name," pled the Duke of Kent, glancing at his wife and the Duke of York.

"What do you suggest?" asked the Archbishop.

"Elizabeth would be . . ."

"No! I won't allow that name," interrupted the Regent fiercely.

Noticing his wife in tears, the Duke of Kent forced himself to keep still.

"Then, what should she be named?" asked the Archbishop. He smiled and spoke quietly in an attempt to smooth the tension.

"Name her Victoria in honor of her mother," snapped the Regent. He spat out the name as if it were distasteful. "But remember Alexandrina comes first!" He underlined his command by staring at the baby.

The Archbishop then baptized the little heir in the name of the Father, the Son and the Holy Ghost.

Her large blue eyes full of wonder, Alexandrina Victoria observed the ceremony without making a sound.

That evening, the Duke and Duchess sponsored a dinner at their apartment in honor of their daughter's christening. The Regent made himself conspicuous by not attending.

The cumbersome name Alexandrina Victoria was soon

shortened by her parents who called her Drina. Then her mother came up with another name she liked better: Vickelchen. The German twist in the name pleased her passion for German sounds.

The little princess gained weight. Her corn-colored hair lengthened every day. The smallpox vaccination weakened her for a time, but soon she became stronger than ever. Often when the family strolled in Hyde Park, the Duke would show her off to a friend and remark, "You've just met a future queen."

People soon formed the habit of going to Kensington Palace, hoping one of the parents would lift little Victoria to the window for them to see. Each time one of them complied, the people responded with a mighty cheer.

The Regent disliked this display. His contempt for his brother increased by the hour. That August, he deliberately lowered the Duke's prestige by openly snubbing him at a reception given by the Spanish Ambassador. He made the snub more obvious when he warmly greeted the Duchess.

Later that month, Madame Siebold was summoned to deliver the nephew of the Duchess of Kent. Her brother's wife, Louise, gave birth to a little prince named Francis Charles Albert Emmanuael, to be called Prince Albert.

3
Providence

Constantly snubbed by the Royal Family, the Duchess of Kent spent many wistful hours tending her little one and trying to suppress her tears. Night after night she sobbed herself to sleep. The language barrier and culture clash rose as formidable obstacles. She continued to have trouble with the letter *V*. Again and again, she would say *wery* instead of very, *voman* instead of woman.

On an emotionally low day, Victoire wiped her tears as she stood at a window. She saw Adelaide step out of her carriage and approach the palace. Delighted, Victoire hurriedly washed her face and hid the handkerchief she had been using.

Soon the two German-born ladies chattered in German over a cup of tea. It was a distinct pleasure for both to be able to express themselves in gutturals again.

Smiling at Victoire, Adelaide confided, "William and I are praying for another baby, e-even th-though . . ." She nervously stirred her tea. "Even though it would place our heir a step ahead of Victoria."

The Duchess of Kent smiled. "We'll leave the matter of succession up to God," she managed. "God *is* sovereign."

A few days later, Adelaide and her husband departed for her beloved Germany. Soon she again announced she expected an heir. Overjoyed, the Duke of Clarence decided their baby should be born in England, just as Victoria had been.

The trip was too much for Adelaide. She miscarried at Calais.

The Duke of Kent, convinced his wife and daughter should escape the chilly palace during the winter, made arrangements to vacation by the sea on the coast of Devonshire.

A week after they moved in, the Duke heard a rifle shot. Terrified that a terrorist might have assassinated his wife, he rushed into her room. She was startled, but all right.

He then peered into Victoria's crib. Horrified, he discovered a bullet had passed through her sleeve. "She was almost killed!" he exclaimed, lifting her up and squeezing her to his chest.

Numb with dismay, Victoire grabbed her and kissed her on each cheek. "Saved by God's providence," she cried. "Yes, she was saved by God's providence. It must be that He has plans for her life!"

A thorough investigation proved the shot had been fired by an innocent young man hunting birds.

One evening, the Duke returned to the cottage, soaked to the skin. "You'd better put on warm shoes and change your clothes," suggested Victoire.

"Oh no. I'm all right," he replied confidently. "I was out with Captain John Conroy inspecting the horses."

"But your feet are soaked. You'll get pneumonia!"

"Don't worry. I'll be all right."

In the morning, he had a fever. Victoire hovered over him. "You'd better let me get you some calomel," she suggested.

Lifting his hands, he replied a little irritably, "I don't need any medicine. When I was in the army I got soaked many times. All I need is rest. Just a little rest."

"How about some James' powder?"

"No."

Victoire put her hand to his forehead. "It will lower your fever."

"Come now, Victoire. Don't pester me."

He continued to worsen so Victoire sent for Dr. Wilson, who decided he should be bled. The doctor applied leeches to Edward's chest and moved his bed into a warmer room. Still his fever continued to rise.

Frantic, the Duchess sent to London for Sir David Dundas, the highly experienced royal physician who had taken care of the Duke in his childhood. Sir David replied that due to the King's illness, he would be unable to come. He sent Dr. William Maton in his stead.

As Victoire waited and prayed, little eight-month old Victoria came down with a severe cold. Victoire shuffled from crib to bed. In her concern for her two loved ones, she neglected to change her clothes for five days.

Maton arrived. As Victoire's limited English clashed with his smattering of French, the two found it almost impossible to communicate.

Holding her breath, Victoire watched with dismay as he bled her husband. Six full pints hadn't satisfied him. She watched in horror as the Doctor selected a cup and a knife. After making an incision, Maton placed a heated four-ounce cup over the wound. As the cup cooled, a vacuum formed and the blood flowed.

The Duke still did not improve, so the Doctor cupped him on various parts of his body. To relieve the Duke's headache, he cupped him on his head also.

By Thursday, the Duke's condition had so deteriorated messengers were sent to Prince Leopold and other relatives to come.

Additional bleeding and blisters did not help the Duke to improve. His temperature soared.

On Sunday morning, January 23, 1820, the Duchess knelt by the side of her husband and held his hand. Just as the clocks struck ten, he took his final breath.

She sighed through her weariness, holding on to one satisfaction; her husband had made his peace with God. *He had even expressed a desire to shake the Regent's hand!*

As she placed the still hand of her husband upon his chest, she rose and went to her daughter. As she held her to her bosom, small tears made their way down her face. "Vick-elchen," she whispered. "How long will they let us stay in Kensington Palace? How am I to feed you, my darling? We are now penniless."

The Duchess turned her body from side to side in a gentle rocking motion, thinking, praying. "Dear God. Please help me. Please help us."

Embalmers prepared the remains of the Duke of Kent and placed them in a huge coffin that weighed over a ton.

Victoire and her baby returned to London with Prince Leopold. The rough ride upset Victoria with frightful jolting. As Victoire comforted her baby, she turned to Leopold. "I think I should return to Germany."

"That would be a mistake," replied Leopold.

"Why?"

"You are the mother of Victoria. And there are chances that she will attain the throne." Leopold stared out the window, pondering his next words. "King George is near death. That means the Regent will become George IV." Leopold sighed.

"That means my little Vickelchen will be closer to the throne."

Leopold nodded. "The next in line is the Duke of York, who is childless. Following him is the Duke of Clarence, who would serve as William IV. If he and Adelaide have an heir, their child would be next in line."

"But if they don't. . . ."

Leopold leaned forward to hold Victoire's hand in his. "You should remain in England even if the Regent would give his right arm to persuade you to return to your old home."

Victoire sat up taller. "Then I'm going to stay!" She slumped a little as a new thought pressed into her mind. "That is, I'll stay if I can find a place to live. And if Parliament will provide me with an income."

"Leave that to me. I'll see you through."

Victoire patted her brother's hand. "Thank you," she murmured. "Thank you very much."

On January 29, the day Victoire and little Victoria moved back to Kensington Palace, eighty-one-year-old George III passed away. His final services took place five days after those of the Duke of Kent.

Shortly after the funeral, the Regent—now George IV—was stricken with pleurisy. Credit for his recovery was given to the doctors who drained more than nine pints of blood from his body.

The grim-reaper in the ranks of the Royal Family did not rest. On August 6, the Duchess of York passed away. Terribly concerned about the succession, George IV urged his brother to remarry. He refused. This pushed Victoria one half step closer to the throne.

The Duchess of Kent continued to sink into debt in spite of getting closer to becoming mother of a queen.

Leopold appealed to the King, who replied, "I won't give her a sixpence." He grinned with sinister satisfaction.

Parliament, however, agreed the Duchess could continue to draw the six thousand pounds a year which had been paid to her husband. Since this was not enough for her to maintain the living standards of a Duchess, Leopold agreed to contribute three thousand pounds a year to help educate Victoria.

Still snubbed by most of the Royal Family, Victoire continued to live in a state of depression until Adelaide renewed her visits.

During one visit, the Duchess set down her cup of tea and leaned forward in her chair. "Now that you are only one step from becoming Queen, aren't you afraid to keep visiting me?" asked the Duchess.

"Ach, no! Ve vimmin from Deuchland must stick togedder," she replied staunchly.

Speaking in German, Victoire asked, "You aren't afraid of offending the King or your husband?"

Adelaide lifted her chin. "Certainly not. I have a leetle surprise for dem."

"Surprise?"

"Yah. I dink I'm going to have another baby."

Victoire tried to hide her shock. "When?"

"In January."

Victoire forced herself to sound cheerful. "That's wonderful."

"Yah. Ve are very happy. Do pray dat ve von't have any drubbles."

"That I will."

Adelaide's daughter came into the world six weeks ahead of time. In spite of her early arrival, the little heiress was in good health. The King was delighted. Her birth meant that Victoria had been pushed back to fourth place in the line of succession.

Indeed, His Majesty was so delighted he made no objections when, during the christening ceremonies, the names Elizabeth and Georgiana were included in the official name.

When the Duchess of Kent learned about this, she withheld her comments.

On March 4, 1821, tiny Elizabeth passed away at St. James's Palace. She was stricken with an "entanglement of the bowels."

Upon hearing the news, Victoire hurried to Adelaide. Arm about her shoulders, she comforted, "It is quite probable that the Lord will send you another child."

"But this is my *second* heartbreak." She wiped her tears.

"Yes, I know. Nevertheless, God *is* sovereign. He knows best!"

"Of course. Still, it's hard to take."

The two duchesses remained very fond of each other. They continued their habit of visiting one another's apartments to share their troubles and to pray and study the German Bible together. Both loved the writings of Martin Luther, especially his hymns. Sometimes they stood together and sang *A Mighty Fortress Is Our God*.

One foggy morning, while Victoire continued in her depth of depression over the loss of her husband, she received a note from Adelaide. In it, a special sentence wrapped itself around her heart. "My children are dead," she scrawled in

German. "But yours lives and she is mine too."

Victoire never forgot that note.

On June 5, the King's absent wife, Princess Caroline Amelia Elizabeth, landed at Dover. She wore a puce colored sarcenet pelisse lined with ermine and a white willow hat. She loved the conflict her appearance caused. She had come to be crowned Queen of England.

His Majesty, King George IV, had frantically tried to stop the inevitable. The Cabinet, after an urgent session, had decided to grant "this infamous woman" an annuity of fifty thousand pounds, payable *"only during her residence abroad."* They felt fifty thousand pounds a year was a cheap price to avoid the scandal that would erupt if the woman were to be made Queen, or if the King pursued a divorce.

The masses, on the other hand, were divided. Upon her appearance, some went wild. They followed her to her place of lodging. After the crowds tired of cheering, they scattered down the streets and systematically smashed the windows of those who had not shown sufficient enthusiasm.

In most of the churches in the United Kingdom, there were many who were unhappy because the Book of Common Prayer did not include prayers for the Queen. Invariably, after the prayer for the Royal Family had been read, a loud but pious voice would add, "And bless the Queen too."

Since the Coronation Committee realized Parliament could do nothing to stop Caroline, they decided to ignore the problem and planned for the coronation ceremonies to take place on July 18.

Tension filled the air that July morning. Fearing Caroline might try to force her way through one of the Abbey doors, they stationed broad shouldered pugilists at each entrance.

Caroline ignored advice that she should not make an appearance. After being turned away from every door, Lord Hood presented her with an admission ticket that carried the distinguished signature: Wellington. "That will get you in," he confided. "But it is only good for one person." He frowned at the ladies with her.

Caroline turned crimson. "I'm the Queen!" she stormed. She spoke so loudly, those nearby stared. "As Queen I should be allowed to be accompanied by these friends of mine." She gestured toward Lady Wood and Lady Hamilton.

"I'm indeed sorry," replied Lord Hood, bowing low. "The Coronation Committee wrote the regulations."

Caroline glanced at the pugilists guarding the door. Fiercely choking back tears, she returned to her lodgings.

The next night, Caroline didn't feel well. Following supper, she poured a tumbler of water, then stirred in some magnesia. She continued adding the drug until the concoction resembled heavy cream. Next, in order that she might sleep, she laced the preparation with opium.

When the "Queen" finally awoke at noon, she was quite ill.

By the following Friday, the doctors considered her case so serious they drained four pints of blood from her arms. This treatment did not help. She gradually sank and finally passed away on August 7.

In order not to embarrass the King, the "Queen's" funeral procession arranged to wind through the back-streets, the planned route kept semisecret. Even so, many turned out to pay their respects. Some were heard to murmur, "God bless Queen Caroline."

His Majesty, George IV, did not attend the funeral. He did wear a black mourning crape on his left arm. In spite of everything, Caroline was the mother of Charlotte, his only legal heir.

Two months after the "Queen" died, Adelaide called on Victoire. "William has just confided to me dat da King is going to fodder his own heir," she said.

"His mistresses are too old for that!" scoffed Victoire. "Besides, they don't have Royal blood."

"Dat's true and he knows it. He's now looking for a princess. He's already studying the lists of awailable ones."

Victoire forced a smile. "He's nearly sixty and he's *huge*!"

"True. But remember, da princess he marries will be da

Queen of Great Britain! He's already on a diet!"

"A diet? Really?"

"Yah. He's on a diet. My husband told me he's already lost a lot of veight."

Victoire put her hands to her mouth. "I hope he loses at least one hundred pounds," she managed. "And I hope it stays off. Still, I wonder if any of the princesses will have him, especially young princesses."

Both of them laughed. But Victoire's laugh was a little uneasy.

4
I Will Be Good

Tiny Victoria spent her earliest days crawling on a specially spread yellow rug. The various bishops who knelt to play with her brought screams of terror from the small child. The wigs and aprons they wore seemed to frighten her.

Victoire grew increasingly dissatisfied with her English. So she invited Reverend George Davys to read English to her. A very mild man who led services in the palace chapel, he had a special love for the poor. This impressed the Duchess to such an extent that she requested he be assigned to instruct Victoria.

Victoria began her studies with him when she was four. He devised his own system to teach her to read. He would take a set of words from a box and place them in various parts of the room. Then he would say, "Victoria, my dear, show me the word *dog*." Victoria would roam around the room, study each word and at last, triumphantly point to the right one. Davys would praise her for her accomplishment. This little fun game proved its effectiveness—she was soon reading simple books.

Victoria impressed Davys with her kindness and generosity. She had over one hundred beautiful dolls, along with many other toys. She liked to lend them or even give them away.

Like other employees, Davys obeyed the instruction to never allow Victoria to learn that someday she might become the Queen. Nonetheless, the little tot soon discovered she was someone special. While toddling along with her nurse and half sister Feodora, she had a question. "Nurse, why do all the gentlemen raise their hats to me and not to Feodora?"

Unable to answer without lying or revealing the truth, the frightened nurse shifted Victoria's attention to a bird that had just lighted on the fence.

Generally, Victoria was happy and smiling. But sometimes she would stamp her foot and demand her own way. Moreover, she seldom had any remorse over what she had said or done. While listening to her mother tell a friend that she had just been through "a little storm," Victoria interrupted her. "Yes," she gloated, "one at dressing and another at washing."

On another occasion, the Duchess lashed out, " Victoria, when you are naughty, you make *me* and *yourself* very unhappy."

"No, Mamma," contradicted Victoria triumphantly, "not *me*, not *myself*, but you!"

Victoria thoroughly enjoyed creating storms, and the more they upset those around her, the better she liked it. She was quick to admit this, for she had determined that she would never tell a lie.

Victoire had decided that her little heir should accept the Lord early in childhood. Because of this firm desire, they shared a pew every Sunday morning. Victoria, sitting silently beneath her broad hat, found it difficult to listen while the pastor preached, "And now, fifteenly . . ." She sat, sure she would melt in the heat, not being allowed to scratch. But she always managed to stay awake, even when the pastor's sermon was unusually long. She accomplished this feat because she knew that later in the afternoon, her mother would quiz her about various points in the sermon.

When Victoria turned five, her mother employed Fraulein Lehzen to move into Kensington Palace and teach her daughter. Louise Lehzen was the daughter of a Lutheran pastor in

Coburg. Her employment raised a storm of ridicule. The Duchess ignored the critics. Fraulein Lehzen had previously served as governess to her daughter Feodora. Victoire was completely satisfied with her, even though she had a passion for caraway seeds.

Victoria had other teachers. Preacher Davys continued to give her lessons in Latin; John Sale provided instruction in music even though she did not respond well to the subject; Mr. Westall developed her talent in drawing and Madame Boudin coached her in walking and dancing gracefully. Victoria's intense love for opera provided the inspiration to learn Italian on her own. Others helped her master French and English.

Lehzen felt an intense challenge to aid her little tenderfoot to develop into a well-balanced person. She viewed her with the same passion Michelangelo must have felt when he first encountered the discarded block of marble from which he carved David. Although not famous for her own tact, Lehzen knew how to cultivate that trait in Victoria. Being with Victoria during many hours of the day, Lehzen had ample opportunity to notice both her good and bad traits.

Victoria's awareness of being mysteriously different than others unfolded with the years. When she was six, Lady Jane Ellice, another playmate her own age, came to the palace for a visit. In the midst of their fun, Victoria cautioned her guest not to touch certain treasured toys. "They are mine," she said. "And I may call you Jane, but you must never call me Victoria."

Puzzled, Lehzen did not know what to do to sand off this rough edge. She found an opportunity a year later while she helped Victoria dress the one hundred and twenty-two puppets they had copied from the characters in the opera *Kenilworth*.

While Victoria cut the blue garter ribbon for the Earl of Leister, she asked, "Fraulein Lehzen, when I was a tiny girl, the Bishop of Salisbury used to let me play with his badge. Mamma told me the badge indicated he is the Chaplain of the Order of the Garter. What is the Order of the Garter?"

"The Most Nobel Order of the Garter was founded by King

Edward III in 1349. The story is that as he danced with the Countess of Salisbury, her garter fell off. While he picked it up, he noticed several people smirking. This made him very angry. So he exclaimed in French, 'shame to him who evil thinks.' He then vowed he would make the blue garter so glorious everyone would wish to wear it."

"Did he?"

"Yes, Victoria. He did. Today it's the highest military honor anyone can receive. Just twenty-five men are allowed to have it at one time. Only the King or Queen can decide who receives this honor."

"Could Uncle King give it to someone?"

"Of course, His Majesty King George IV can give it to anyone he likes."

Victoria's eyes widened. "Could he give it to Uncle Leopold?"

"Certainly. But he couldn't give it to him unless there were fewer than twenty-five members at the time."

"Why is it such a wonderful honor?"

"It is a great honor, Victoria, because the best thing anyone can do is help others. King Edward helped that woman. Jesus said, 'And whosoever will be chief among you, let him be your servant.' "

Victoria frowned. "What does that mean?"

"It means that if we have the opportunity to help others, we should help them."

"Does that mean that I should help the poor little girls who don't have as many toys as I have?"

"It does."

"I already gave Lady Jane Ellice one of my dolls. Does that mean I'll be a member of that order?"

Trying not to smile, Fraulein Lehzen replied, "You, Victoria, are already a member of the order, even though you are not among the special twenty-five."

Victoria pushed her lips together in confusion, then asked. "How could I be a member? I'm only seven."

"You are a member because you are related to both King George I and King George II. All of their descendants are members. Of course, as a girl, you are merely a lady of that order."

"Since I'm a member, what must I do?"

"You must be kind to everyone, even the servants. And remember you have a special obligation to be good."

"Why?"

"Because your grandfather is a King and your grandmother is a Queen. The French say, 'noblesse oblige.' That means the nobility have the obligation to be generous."

"Then I'm going to be generous," replied Victoria, nodding her head.

Victoria had just begun to make a pencil drawing of Lehzen when her mother approached, catching up Victoria's hands in her own. "His Majesty has invited all of us to visit him at the Royal Lodge," she said excitedly. "This is a great honor and I want you to be dressed just right."

Victoria put away her pencil and paper. "When I speak to him, should I address him as Your Majesty, King George the Fourth?"

"Oh, no." Her mother laughed. "Just call him Uncle King, for he is your father's oldest brother. Be very polite and be sure to curtsey."

"I thought he didn't like us."

"Maybe he's changed his mind."

After she had been dressed and her hair curled, Victoria studied herself in the full-length mirror. She winked one of her blue eyes and spun around in her blue dress. She giggled at the leaf of holly that had been fastened to the neck of her dress to remind her to keep her chin up. As a final gesture, she stuck out her tongue.

Victoria sat in the front of the coach with Lehzen while her mother shared a seat with Feodora. During the journey, Victoria turned to her mother. "Mamma," she inquired, "what will happen if Uncle King dies? Who would then sit on the throne?"

"His brother Frederick, of course."

"Is he the one who gave me the donkey?"

"He is."

"Then I hope he becomes the new king." She was thought-ful for a long moment. Then she asked, "But Mamma, who would be the king after he dies?"

"Your Uncle William."

"Then who would reign after Uncle William?"

The Duchess gulped, licked her lips and adjusted her skirt. As her silence became unbearable, she replied, "Maybe by then Aunt Adelaide will have a baby. If she does, her baby could occupy the throne."

"But tiny babies in diapers can't rule!" scoffed Victoria.

"True. If a baby came to the throne, a regent would be appointed to reign until the baby was eighteen."

"What if the baby is a girl?" persisted Victoria.

"Then she would be the Queen."

Victoria gasped. "Of all England?"

"Yes, all of England and the entire British Empire."

"But what if Aunt Adelaide doesn't have a baby? Or what if she has another baby and it dies like her first two babies died?"

"Victoria, you ask too many questions!" The Duchess pointed out the window. "Look at all those nice cows and horses out there. And look at the beautiful red barn and that stack of hay."

When the carriage arrived at the Royal Lodge, the King took Victoria by the hand, saying, "Give me your little paw." She later wrote:

> He was large and gouty but with a wonderful dignity and charm of manner. He wore the wig which was so much worn in those days. Then he said he would give me something for me to wear, and that was his picture set in diamonds. . . .[1]

Lady Conyngham, the King's current mistress, pinned the glittering miniature on Victoria's shoulder. Victoria beamed with pride. The King then offered his cheek. Repelled by the crimson coat of oily rouge, she barely managed a peck.

---

[1]*Queen Victoria in Her Letters and Journals*, 1985, p. 10.

A day or two later, while Victoria was being driven around the park, she came upon the King in his phaeton. Smiling down upon her, he said, "Pop her in." Lifted by the waist, she wedged between the King and his sister Mary, the Duchess of Gloucester. Victoria recalled:

> Mamma was much frightened. I was greatly pleased and remember that I looked with great respect at the scarlet liveries, etc. We drove around the nicest part of Virginia Water and stopped at the Fishing Temple. . . . The King paid great attention to my sister, and some people fancied he might marry her!! She was very lovely then—about 18—and had charming manners, about which the King was extremely particular.[2]

When His Majesty asked Victoria to request a number for the band to play, she demonstrated that Lehzen's lessons in diplomacy had been most effective. "Ask them to play *God Save the King*," she said.

On the way back to Kensington Palace, Victoria turned to her mother. "Mamma," she asked, "if the king marries a princess will that princess be the Queen?"

"Of course."

"Even if the princess is quite young?"

"Age would make no difference. Why do you ask?"

"Because I'm curious." She spoke evasively while glancing at Feodora out of the corner of her eye.

Feodora blushed.

Providence preceded Victoria all her life. And now that subtle power began to make even more obvious moves. All who watched realized it was determinedly pushing Victoria toward the King's row as if it were playing a game of checkers. Moreover, each move, as subtle as it might be, eventually proved to be perfect.

Victoria had become deeply attached to Louise Lehzen. During a period of illness, Victoria noted in her diary:

> Dear good Lehzen takes such care of me and is so unceasing in her attentions to me that I shall never be able to

---

[2]Ibid.

repay her sufficiently for it but by my love and gratitude. . . .
She is the most affectionate, devoted, attached and disin-
terested friend I have and I love her most dearly. . . .[3]

Victoria's attachment to Lehzen annoyed some of the
bluebloods attached to the palace staff. "She's not only a German and a Lutheran, but she's also a mere commoner," they
scorned. "It isn't right that she should have such influence
over a princess who may become the Queen."

At first the complaints were merely whispers. But the
whispers increased in volume. Soon they became rumbles.
The Duchess was concerned. She loved Lehzen. Still, she
didn't want to unnecessarily annoy the King. Frequently, she
couldn't sleep as she scoured her mind for a solution.

Her solution came through the man who controlled her
finances—Captain John Conroy. He used his connections to
persuade the King to make Lehzen a baroness of Hanover.
And this the King did. This action silenced the critics, for
Baroness Lehzen then had a title just as valid as the titles of
many who complained.

Both Sir John Conroy and the Duchess of Kent now faced
another serious problem. If the King should marry Feodora,
she would be Queen Feodora. If Queen Feodora had a child,
her child would immediately become the heir apparent.

As Sir John pondered this problem, he caressed his heavily starched wing collar and thoughtfully chewed his nails.
He wanted the chance of being in the position to tell the
Duchess, as Regent, what to do. Then he smiled. His cunning
Irish mind had devised a solution. And it was a very simple
one. Princess Feodora needed a husband and she needed one
immediately.

While Conroy consulted lists of available princes, the
Duke of York's continuing illness worsened. He passed away
in January, 1827. This meant that only the King and William
stood between Victoria and the throne. Unless, of course, the
King or Adelaide produced an heir.

If all this was apparent to Victoria, she kept it a secret in
her heart.

---

[3]Ibid, p. 15.

Conroy's romantic efforts proved successful. Toward the final days of 1827, Princess Feodora was married to thirty-two year old Prince Ernest Christian Charles of Hohenlohe Lagenburg. Dressed in lace, Victoria served as bridesmaid.

Victoria loved history, especially the history of British Royal Families. Beginning with the Wessex kings, she could rattle off the various names like the hour-bong of a clock. She was especially familiar with all the rulers in the House of Tudor, the House of Stuart and the House of Hanover. On March 11, 1830, when she was in her eleventh year, she began her history lesson with Louise Lehzen. It was based on *Howlett's Tables* of the kings and queens of England.

As she read, she noticed a new page had mysteriously appeared in the book. "I never saw that page before," she remarked.

"You're right. I just put it in," replied her teacher.

"Why?"

"Because it wasn't necessary for you to see it before."

Frowning, Victoria studied the genealogical chart. It showed all the possible heirs to the throne, together with the dates of their deaths. As she studied, it suddenly became apparent to her that after the deaths of Uncle King and Uncle William she would be the next one to occupy the throne. As this fact gripped her mind, she began to wipe her eyes.

"Why are you crying?" asked Lehzen.

"Because I know what it's like to be the head of the Empire. The responsibilities are terrible." After she dried her eyes, she lifted the forefinger of her right hand and proclaimed, *"I will be good."*

Still under the spell of her discovery, she said, "I understand now why you urged me to learn even Latin . . . you told me Latin is the foundation of English grammar . . ." She then placed her hand solemnly in Lehzen's and firmly repeated, as if making a vow, "I will be good."[4]

In May, George IV was swollen to an enormous size by an

---

[4]*Queen Victoria, Born to Succeed*, 1964, p. 32.

unknown illness. His doctors tapped the soles of his feet in order to drain away the excess water.

His Majesty improved for a few months, then began to deteriorate. The doctors were frantic. Again and again they bled him. Nothing helped. All of England prayed, but without avail. That summer, on the morning of June 26, he burst a blood vessel in his stomach. As he clutched his doctor's hand, he murmured, "My boy, this is death." He was sixty-eight.

At 6 A.M. that morning, a kneeling subject awakened William and informed him that he was now His Majesty, King William the Fourth. Although William had wept at his dying brother's bedside, he had been looking forward to this elevation. Indeed, he had already assured the Duke of Wellington that he hoped Wellington would remain as Prime Minister.

According to gossips, it was reported that the moment he learned that he was the new king, he smirked, "Well, now, I'll be able to kiss the Queen!"

Later, as he was driven to Windsor in the royal coach and heard the crowds singing *God Save the King*, he grinned from ear to ear. Queen Adelaide was not so flippant. Twenty-eight years younger than sixty-five-year-old William, she realized she faced overwhelming responsibilities. She hated being married to a playboy king, already nicknamed Silly Billy.

5

Intrigue

In spite of King William's desire that the Duke of Wellington remain Prime Minister, he was replaced at the end of July 1830 by Earl Grey, a formidable aristocrat. The new Prime Minister arranged an audience with the Duchess of Kent to address three issues.

The Duchess, realizing the King disliked her, had strong misgivings about the meeting.

After a nervous cough, Lord Grey announced the King planned to request Parliament to award her an extra six thousand pounds a year. At this, the Duchess ground her teeth, for the Duke of Wellington had encouraged her to think in terms of twenty thousand pounds. To avoid a confrontation, she replied the subject was too delicate for her immediate comment. The second item was that His Majesty wished her to appoint a lady of "high rank" to be "in attendance" to Princess Victoria. To this, the Duchess agreed. But she said she did not want to announce her choice until *after* Parliament decided the amount of her allowance.

The third item hit with incredible force. "The King," stated the Prime Minister, "wants you to change your daughter's name."

The Duchess stared. "Change her name? Why?"

"Because the name Victoria is foreign."

"Foreign! Do you know who suggested the name Victoria?"

"Who?"

"The King's eldest brother, His Majesty, King George the Fourth, that's who."

Lord Grey shrugged. "Perhaps he didn't realize she would eventually become Queen," he replied, rather lamely. "Nonetheless, His Majesty wants it changed."

"No one should ever change their christened name," protested Victoire.

"It could be changed when she's confirmed."

The Duchess felt herself weakening. Finally she said, "I will write you about the matter."

The Duchess did not write about the matter to the Prime Minister for over a month. In her letter dated January 28, 1831, she explained how the names Alexandrina Victoria were chosen. Then, she continued:

> . . . I cannot conceal from the King that it would grieve me to see my child lay aside the name of Victoria, which she alone uses, as being mine, and, as I mentioned verbally to your Lordship, She has also a great attachment to that name. But, I must look upon this question, as I have taught myself to look upon many others—and be ready to do that which is most suitable to Her Station and the feelings of the Country.
>
> I therefore freely admit that the two foreign names She bears are not suited to our national feeling, and that they should be laid aside.[1]

A week after sending the letter, the Duchess began to worry about what she had done. The story had gotten into the newspapers and the people didn't like it. They felt no one should have to ever change their name, especially a king or queen.

Victoria was also unhappy. "I like my name and I don't want to change it," she announced. "The idea of changing it is just another one of Uncle William's silly ideas."

"But I've already agreed that it should be changed," wailed the Duchess.

[1]*Queen Victoria*, 1921, p. 84.

Victoria became thoughtful. "Have you consulted with the Archbishop of Canterbury?" she asked.

"No."

"Then I would consult him."

In a letter dated June 8, 1831, the Archbishop of Canterbury replied that neither he nor any other bishop was authorized to change a name at the time of confirmation that had been bestowed during christening ceremonies.

Strengthened by this information, the Duchess addressed a letter to the Prime Minister on June 25. She wrote:

> . . . it will be quite contrary to the Princess's and my feelings, if the King persists in changing Her name—and I trust His Majesty may be advised to abandon the intention: I see nothing now, on mature reflection, in its favor but many grave questions against it. . . ."[2]

The next morning while the Duchess and Victoria ate breakfast, the butler laid a silver tray upon the table. The Duchess picked up the letter resting on it. After the butler had bowed himself out of the room, she slit it open.

As Victoria buttered a slice of toast, her mother exclaimed, "Just listen to what the Prime Minister has to say!"

> [I] can not conceal from your Royal Highness my apprehension that it may greatly disappoint His Majesty after the full assent was given by your Royal Highness . . . in your letter of January 28th.[3]

After folding the letter and wedging it between two candlesticks, the Duchess all but shouted, "I don't care whether I've disappointed His Majesty or not. I will not consent for you to have your name changed!" She slapped the table and pursed her lips in determination.

Victoria paused with the toast halfway to her mouth. "But, Mamma, what if he insists?"

"That will make no difference!"

"What if he calls you a traitor and sends you to the Tower?"

"He wouldn't dare. You are the heir presumptive and I am

---

[2]Ibid, p. 85.
[3]Ibid.

your mother. Indeed, I may be the next Regent." She slapped the table again.

"Maybe so. But I would be careful. Thirty-six members of The Most Noble Order of the Garter have been beheaded."

The Duchess laughed. "That was a long time ago. We're living in the nineteenth century! Kings don't cut people's heads off anymore."

Victoria wiped crumbs from her lips. "But they still hang them."

Victoria and her mother both laughed.

Each hoped the King would forget his project. He did not. He replied instantly to the Prime Minister. "His Majesty would not object to the name of Elizabeth . . . his sole aim being the name of the future Sovereign of his country be English . . ."[4]

When Lord Grey explained this to the Duchess, she replied, "The name Elizabeth was suggested at her christening, but King George—I mean the Regent—objected vehemently. If, Lord Grey, the name wasn't good then, it isn't good now. My daughter *will* be Queen Victoria. She will *not* be Queen Elizabeth the Second, even though that is an honorable name."

The Prime Minister shook his head. "His Majesty will be extremely unhappy about your decision."

"I'm sorry about that. But she was christened Alexandrina Victoria and she will remain Alexandrina Victoria. The Archbishop of Canterbury said that neither he nor any other bishop has the right to change a name that has been conferred during a christening."

"It could be changed by Parliament."

"Perhaps. I don't want to argue. She's my daughter and she *will* reign as Queen Victoria."

"Very well, Your Highness. I understand how you feel. I do hope that no problems develop from your decision to disobey His Majesty, the King. Good day."

The date of the coronation of King William and Queen

---

[4]Ibid.

Adelaide approached. England quivered with excitement. Each potential participant planned what to wear, what to say, how to act. All of them eagerly awaited a letter that would inform them exactly what they were to do. Scholars burned their candles late as they decided who would sing in the choir, who would play the organ, who would stand at the doors and how the King and Queen would be dressed. Some participants, like those who would blow the trumpets, were summoned because of ability. Others would be named because of their titles or positions. Many would be chosen because a father had participated in such ceremonies in the past. As the eldest son of this father, they had inherited the right to do the same.

According to tradition, Victoria, as heir presumptive, would follow the King and Queen as they marched down the aisle on September 8, 1831. Dressed in mourning, she had taken this position at the funeral of her uncle, George IV, and now she looked forward to having the same position during the coronation.

As the coronation date approached, the excitement throughout the United Kingdom increased by the hour. Tailors filled their shelves with the finest bolts of cloth, and jewelers kept the diamond cutters in Amsterdam busy. The bankers were also greedy with anticipation, for they knew that many would go into debt in order to buy or rent the finest jewels and costumes that could be obtained.

Victoria sometimes became so excited she found it hard to sleep. In order to pass the time, she decided to draw an elaborate portrait of Baroness Lehzen. As Victoria worked at her easel, the Duchess sat in a chair and watched.

Skillfully, Victoria drew her teacher's dark, slightly almond eyes, perfectly curved brows, thin, triangular nose and firm chin. Finally, with loving touches, she began to frame her slender face with dark puffs of hair that extended just below her ears.

"You really love Lehzen, don't you?" commented the Duchess.

"Yes, Mamma, I certainly do. She's a great teacher."

"Victoria, I have something important that I want to say to you."

The ominous tone in her mother's voice caused Victoria to pause as she darkened the hair just below Lehzen's ear.

"Yes, Mamma. I'm listening."

"You've become so attached to Lehzen, you study in her room, go with her for long walks and share books together. And, I suppose, you even confide in her."

"So?"

"One of these days your uncle William will be gone. The moment he's gone you will be Queen Victoria. But remember, you won't be able to reign until you are eighteen."

"Go on."

"And so, I'll probably have to serve as Regent."

"Yes."

"And so I think you'd better spend more time with me than with Lehzen."

"Why?"

"So that we can learn to work together. As it is, Lehzen knows you better than I know you."

After her mother had gone, Victoria started working on the black ribbon that circled her teacher's neck and drooped beneath a broach to the center of her chest. But a flood of tears stopped her before she could finish.

Rushing into her room, Victoria threw herself on the bed and sobbed. She loved both her mother and her governess. Each meant more to her than life. The fact that her mother seemed jealous horrified her. In the midst of her tears, she thought of her uncle Leopold. *If only he were here, he would tell her what to do!* Unfortunately, her mother's brother was away on a trip. In a way, she considered him a substitute father. She also regarded him as a very wise man.

Only a week later, another blow fell on Victoria. A letter from the Prime Minister arrived. As her mother read it, her face whitened. "Listen to this, Victoria," she said. "The Prime Minister has informed me the King has decided you cannot march behind him during the coronation ceremonies."

Victoria's smile vanished. "Then where am I to march?"

"Behind the dukes."

"But I'm the heir presumptive!" exclaimed Victoria.

"That's true. And it isn't right."

Victoria sighed. Then, her eyes on the floor, she asked, "Mamma, I know this is very personal, but could anyone claim that I'm not legitimate?"

"Certainly not! I have royal blood and your father had royal blood. You were born right here in Kensington Palace. The Archbishop of Canterbury, along with other high officials verified your birth. Had you been born five days later, you would have been born on our wedding anniversary."

As the date for the coronation ceremonies drew close, Victoria kept wondering what she would wear and the position in which she would march. Her mother still prayed the King would change his mind and allow her daughter to march right behind himself—the position called for by tradition. But His Majesty held on to his stubbornness. "Although Victoria is the heir presumptive," he repeated, "she will march behind the dukes."

Disgusted, as well as dismayed, the Duchess decided to be as stubborn as the King. "If he will not let Victoria take her rightful place, then we will not attend the coronation ceremonies," she informed the Prime Minister.

"Your Highness, that would be dreadful," he replied.

"Dreadful or not, we *won't* attend."

After the Prime Minister had gone, Victoria put her arms around her mother. "Mamma," she begged. "Please change your mind."

"No, we will not attend," replied her mother, and the issue was settled.

Victoria wept. Nothing could console her, not even her dolls.

On coronation morning, Victoria tiptoed to the closet and studied the beautiful gown she would have worn had she been allowed to attend. Sewn by the best seamstresses in London, it symbolized her purity and station in life as heir apparent. Relying on imagination, she visualized herself marching behind the King and Queen; heard the exquisite tones of the great organ; saw the flashing diamonds, rubies and sapphires; smelled the expensive perfume radiating from the richest women in the kingdom, and felt the heavy carpet beneath her feet.

Suddenly her eyes overflowed. *Why did her mother and the King have to be so stubborn?* In Shakespeare's lines, it was "Much Ado About Nothing." As she thought about it, she made a firm resolve that when she became Queen, she would remember that trivia was trivia.

Surrounded by that which is artificial—smiles, conversations, flattery—Victoria longed for that which is true and simple. Her favorite sermons were preached by men who emphasized, "Behold, now is the day of salvation."

One afternoon in the fall, while the leaves turned brown, Victoria went to a gypsy camp near Claremont. The crude wagons and smiling faces were a pleasant contrast to what she had endured at Kensington Palace. Conversing with these olive-skinned, dark-eyed people pleased her. They loved their wagons, their children, their manner of life. None went out of the way to make an impression. She admired their genuine love for children and the elderly.

Victoria enjoyed every moment of her visit. Having learned they needed food and blankets, she had these items sent to them. She also considered ways that would provide an education for their children.

The memory of the gypsy camp lingered in her heart. Back in the coldness of the palace, faced with artificiality, Victoria longed for the simplicity of the gypsies. She discovered Crabbe's *Gipsie's Advocate* in the library. She and Lehzen read the book together while Lehzen munched caraway seeds. From this book and her memories, Victoria became convinced that the poor tended to experience more of the *real* joys of life than the rich.

As the months shuffled by, the Duchess of Kent and John Conroy became more and more domineering. The Duchess insisted on sharing Victoria's room, even though there were many other rooms. She also insisted on sitting with Victoria when she studied and going with her on walks. Previously, Lehzen had read to her when she combed her hair. Now, her mother insisted on reading to her.

Victoria was annoyed. She loved her mother, but she didn't want to be shadowed. Moreover, Lehzen was her governess.

One afternoon, when her unhappiness with her mother and John Conroy reached a peak, she accidentally entered an unlocked room and saw them standing in each other's arms. Shocked, Victoria managed to keep still.

Then, like a detective, Victoria searched for additional information. Soon she discovered her mother and Sir John always spoke about the King's health. She also noticed gleams of satisfaction on their faces when reports said the King did not feel well. All at once, the solution to her questions became clear. *They anticipated the possibility that the King would die before she became eighteen. If that happened, her mother would be the Regent and Sir John would tell her what to do!*

Suddenly, Victoria felt sick to her stomach. Long ago she had prayed that she might love everyone. Now she found it difficult to have any love, or even a shred of respect, for Conroy. In the depths of her heart, she decided that when she became Queen she would deal with him.

Knowledge of what her mother and John Conroy had in mind mixed with memories of the atrocities of Queen Mary and Queen Elizabeth. The mixture thoroughly disillusioned her. She felt as if she suffered from acute food poisoning. *Was anyone honest? Did anyone have pure motives?*

As she prepared for her religious examination by the Archbishop of Canterbury, she spent hours studying the Sermon on the Mount. The wonderful words of Jesus made her heart soar. But it seemed that none of those who had reigned before, defenders of the faith though they were, had even attempted to follow the teachings of Jesus. Nor did any of those around her, with the possible exception of Lehzen and Preacher Davys.

That afternoon as Victoria pondered her lessons of the morning, she thought of her future as Queen and Defender of the Faith. As she remembered the words of Jesus, she decided she would be different than those around her. She would *defend* the faith, not simply sit back and let evil take the reins of control over the kingdom.

6

Royal Apprenticeship

V ictoria's examination by the bishops proved that she was doing well. They reported, ". . . in answering a great variety of questions . . . the Princess displayed an accurate knowledge of the most important features of Scripture, History and of the leading truths and precepts of the Christian Religion as taught by the Church of England, as well as an acquaintance with the Chronology and principal facts of English History, remarkable in so young a person. To questions in Geography, the use of the Globes, Arithmetic and Latin Grammar, the answers which the Princess returned were equally satisfactory."[1]

Having mastered these basics, Victoria needed to understand the governing process of England. Fortunately for her, the Reform Bill sat in front of Parliament as their newest concern. Laced with controversy, this proposed legislation seized the attention of everyone in the United Kingdom. Day after day, voters eagerly read the headlines and cartoons.

The major problem was the electoral process in Parliament. Victoria studied the newspapers. Authorities from Parliament and her teachers briefed her.

"You see, Your Royal Highness," explained Davys, "the In-

---

[1]*The Young Victoria*, p. 80.

dustrial Revolution changed everything. This is because workers tend to leave the vast country estates and move to the industrial centers where they can earn their living at the mills."

"Why do they move?" Victoria asked.

"Because they can earn more money spinning cotton than they can by weeding gardens, tending sheep, or plowing fields. This migration has been so great, Birmingham, Leeds and Manchester now have a combined population of half a million. Yet the places where people left, like Old Sarum or the county of Cornwall, have extremely small populations."

"So?" Victoria asked, not understanding why this should be important.

"One of the problems is that Old Sarum still has two seats in Parliament just as it did when it was heavily populated; and the county of Cornwall still has forty-four seats, even though only a few people live there. But Birmingham, Leeds and Manchester, even though they are literally jammed with workers, have no representatives in Parliament at all."

Victoria frowned. "That's terrible."

"Of course it is. And the problem is getting worse. In 1760, when your grandfather came to the throne, the total population of England, Scotland and Wales was only eight million. Now it is sixteen and a half million. Yet the number of delegates in Parliament is exactly the same as it was then." Victoria positioned her arms across her chest. A stern, queenly look enveloped her face. "That will have to be changed."

"Yes, our system must be changed. The county of Cornwall must relinquish some of its seats, while Birmingham, Leeds and Manchester should be given seats. The mill workers are demanding representation. These changes will be difficult to accomplish. It will be like extracting all a man's teeth on the same day."

"If it's the right thing to do, why will it be hard?"

"Because human beings are corrupt. 'Rotten boroughs' like Old Sarum are owned by rich men. The owners dictate to their tenants how to vote. If they don't obey, the owners get rid of them." Davys rubbed his beard. He turned from Victoria and frowned. "The rich control Parliament. Seats in Parliament can be bought, sold or even inherited. It's a vicious system."

Victoria rested her chin in her hands, looking intently at the pacing Davys. "What does the Reform Bill propose to do?"

"It proposes to allow more people to vote and to apportion the delegates more fairly. Parliament has a horrendous problem on its hands. You and I have ringside seats from which we can watch the struggle and see how government works."

Victoria stood up and pressed her hands on the table. She leaned forward, excited about the opportunity.

Davys said the whole country was watching. "Boroughs all over England that are not being represented are demanding action. But I'm afraid I must leave you now and begin working on a sermon."

"What are you going to preach about?"

"God's providence."

While Parliament readied for the tug of war, Victoria continued her studies. One story especially intrigued her. In 1588, Queen Elizabeth faced an insurmountable problem when King Philip II sent his Armada to conquer England. His ships, Victoria learned, were much larger, better equipped and more numerous than the English ships.

On July 18, as the Spanish ships approached the English coast, the fears of the people sent them to their knees. England had not seen the campfires of an invader since 1066. And the Spanish, they knew, were determined. They were determined to avenge the death of Mary, Queen of Scots and to turn England back to Roman Catholicism.

Queen Elizabeth had confidence that her navy would do well even though her ships were much smaller. But in this time of peril, she knew that England could only be saved by God's providence. With this in mind, she asked her chaplain to write a prayer of intercession to be read all over England. Victoria's eyes glistened as she slowly read that prayer which began:

> O Lord God, heavenly Father, the Lord of Hosts, without
> whose providence nothing proceedeth, and without whose
> mercy nothing is saved. . . .[2]

Victoria reread the entire prayer, then continued with the rest of the story. She learned that instead of her kingdom being handicapped by her smaller ships, the smaller ships proved to be an advantage, since they could easily be maneuvered. Skillfully they followed the large Spanish galleons and bombarded them with cannons from a safe distance—in the manner of small birds plucking feathers from the tail of a hawk. Next, they crammed seven ships with combustibles and sent them without crews into the midst of the Armada.

The fire-ships stayed together as if they were being guided by an unseen hand and caused great damage to the enemy fleet. On July 28, the commander of the Armada admitted defeat and headed home by way of the Orkney islands north of Scotland.

The United Kingdom was jubilant. But many worried that the Armada would gather reinforcements and return. Concerned that her men would not become overconfident or discouraged, Queen Elizabeth decided that she would leave the safety of London and go to the front.

"Your Majesty," exclaimed a horrified advisor, "you may be assassinated!"

"Nonsense. God will take care of me," replied the Queen.

On August 8, Queen Elizabeth stepped into a barge and headed east on the Thames. As she neared the riverfront of Tilbury Fort, she dressed for the occasion. White, she had decided, would be her theme. The angels in the empty tomb had worn white and so would she! She dressed in white velvet, put on a gleaming breastplate of silver and carried a silver truncheon trimmed in gold.

The Earl of Leicester met her at the riverfront of Tilbury Fort. He had with him a regiment of foot soldiers and a large cavalry escort. Hatless, the Queen mounted a white horse. Preceded by two pages who carried her silver helmet on a

[2]*Elizabeth I, A Study of Power and Intellect*, pp. 313–314.

white pillow, she rode to the fort. There she inspected the troops. While columns of men knelt, she read her speech of encouragement.

That day at dinner, it was rumored that the Armada was returning. But it did not return. As it sailed, furious storms caught the fleet. Only fifty ships limped back to Spain.

Other than the seven fire-ships, England lost only one ship. It was a miraculous victory.

Elizabeth's words in her prayer and speech enchanted Victoria. Victoria dreamed of Elizabeth's courage and the white velvet she wore to the fort. Victoria sat, staring out her window, impressed with how Elizabeth had honored the Lord and the way the United Kingdom had been saved by God's providence.

The next day, Victoria forced her mind away from Philip and Elizabeth to the Reform Bill, which was first debated before Lord Grey became Prime Minister.

The initial skirmish over the bill came in the House of Commons when the Duke of Wellington, who was Prime Minister at that time, and an opponent of the bill, said, "I am fully convinced that the country possesses at the moment a legislature which answers all the good purposes of legislation." When the Duke sat down, a stunned silence followed him.

Victoria had learned how Wellington was forced to resign, and the people elected a Whig, Lord Grey, to be Prime Minister.

"Reverend Davys, what's a Whig?"

"The word *whig* is a shortened form of the Scottish word *whiggamore* which meant 'a driver of horses.' The Whigs believe the people should have more power. The Tories believe that the King should have more power. I believe your mother is a Whig. Your Uncle William is a Tory."

In addition to being an excellent speaker, Lord Grey was a clever diplomat. Whigs comprised most of his cabinet. But he diplomatically appointed a Tory, the Duke of Richmond, to the important position of Postmaster General.

Grey knew the King was against the Reform Bill, but he was convinced that if he used the best strategy, he could maneuver it through both the House of Commons and the House of Lords and have it signed into law.

Debate on the measure had gone on for a long time. If the bill passed, it would mean sixty rotten boroughs would lose both members. Forty-seven others would lose one member. Seats would then be distributed to boroughs with a population over ten thousand. All men of legal age would be allowed to vote if their income was at least ten pounds a year.

When all these details were first revealed, the Tories responded with ironical laughter, and some of the Whigs shouted, "They're mad! They're mad!"

The response worried Prime Minister Grey. Perhaps, he thought, if the bill is not passed, the King should dismiss Parliament and call for new elections. King William, however, was not interested. He feared a general election would increase tensions throughout the nation to an exploding point. Rumors that some workers had already armed themselves filtered through the country.

The second reading of the bill in the House of Commons passed by a very narrow margin, 302–301.

"What happens next?" Victoria asked Davys.

Davys shrugged. "The bill may squirm through the House of Commons, but there is so much opposition it will die in the House of Lords."

"Then what will they do?"

"If that should happen, and it probably will, the King can appoint new peers to the House of Lords. By doing that, he can get a majority of them on his side."

A few days after the close vote, the King dismissed three officers from his household because they had voted against the bill. This upset Victoria. "Is the King really for the bill?" she all but demanded.

Davys shrugged. "I think Uncle William is really against it." Victoria cocked her head and looked wise.

Davys shrugged again. But this time a tiny smile played

on his lips. Victoria shoved the newspaper aside. "Do you think the King will terminate Parliament?"

"Prorogue it? Never!"

The Reform Bill became the subject of conversation everywhere. The workers were solidly for it. Most of the lords, especially those who owned rotten boroughs, were against it. To them, the whole idea was "simply shocking." The polarization continued to increase all during the spring and early summer.

While having breakfast one day, the King suddenly made up his mind to deal with the problem. He summoned his coach and went to the House of Lords.

Immense confusion ruled in the House of Lords that day. When the King arrived, the sight of him calmed the confusion. His Majesty strode to the throne, plunked himself down and glared at the all-but-stunned lords before him. He then announced that parliament was prorogued.

This announcement so shocked the Tories, many of them could do nothing but stare. After regaining his composure, a lord who owned several rotten boroughs approached another owner of rotten boroughs. "Is His Majesty for the bill or is he not?" he demanded while adjusting his monocle.

"I don't know," replied his frustrated friend. "All I know is that we are living in perilous times. Just imagine some h-dropping Cockney with an income of only ten pounds a year being allowed to vote. Sure, we need some reform. But we don't need to turn the world upside down!"

"What does all this mean?" inquired Victoria.

"Your Royal Highness, it means that we should pray," replied Davys. "The United Kingdom is on the verge of Civil War. Thanks to the Christian revivals of the Wesleys, England escaped the carnage of the French Revolution. God's providence is still at work. Let's pray that the right people will be elected in the coming election."

"That I will," replied Victoria.

7

Barefoot Queen

Victoria followed the political events closely. Riots broke out. The King refused to create new peers so the Reform Bill would pass.

"Is that the end of the bill?" questioned Victoria at the beginning of her lesson.

"Certainly not," replied Davys. "I don't know what the course of events will be. But I do know this one thing. If the bill is pleasing to God, it will be passed. Never forget providence!"

The battle over the bill and its wording continued. In a last-resort move, Grey assembled his cabinet and took them to see the King.

The King listened reluctantly, then finally gave in. "Well, now it must be so, and I consent," he said.[1]

"Will you put your decision on paper?" asked Brougham.[2]

The King scowled. "Do you doubt my word?" He then went to a desk and wrote:

> His Majesty authorizes Earl Grey, if any obstacle should arise during the further progress of the Bill, to submit to

[1]*William IV*, 1980, p. 164.
[2]*Lord Grey of the Reform Bill*, 1920, p. 348.

him a creation of Peers to such extent as shall be necessary to carry the Bill.[3]

With this threat hanging over their heads, the lords abandoned their opposition. On June 4, 1832, the third reading was passed by a majority of 106 to 22. Most of the Tory seats were empty. Unwilling to vote for legislation they hated, they stayed away.

The miraculous passage of this legislation put England in a festive mood. Immensely pleased, Victoria discussed the victory with her mother. "I learned a lot about politics," she said. "And I am now convinced, more than ever, that God's providence is the most important element."

As Victoria grew taller and began to bloom into womanhood, she became more convinced of the power of prayer. Tired of being ordered about, she sometimes found it difficult not to hate both her mother and John Conroy.

Often, after a painful confrontation with her mother or Conroy, Victoria fled to her room and tried to relax with a book. Even then, her mother generally barged in and stretched out on the other bed. Utterly frustrated, Victoria felt like an animal in the zoo. She thought of David and sympathized with him when he cried out, "Oh that I had wings like a dove! For then I would fly away and be at rest" (Ps. 55:6).

Victoria became interested in the problem of slavery when she received a model of the slave ship Brookes as a gift. Wanting to know more, she found a biography of Queen Elizabeth and began to read.

She smiled when she learned Good Queen Bess had been horrified when informed that Sir John Hawkins had transported slaves from Africa to the New World. She declared that this was "detestable and would call down the vengeance of heaven."

Victoria's joy didn't last.

---

[3]Ibid.

As she turned the pages, she learned the Queen's reaction didn't deter Sir John. The hard-hearted sea captain sharpened his beard and took his account book to the palace. Intrigued by the "easy" money, Queen Elizabeth decided the transportation of slaves wasn't detestable after all. Indeed, she lent Sir John the 700-ton Jesus of Lubeck, a ship larger than all the ships of Columbus combined. As the head of the Church of England and Defender of the Faith, the Queen soothed her conscience by assuming the Trade would expose slaves to Christianity.

Sick at heart, Victoria closed the book with a bang. Sitting up she stretched her stiff muscles. Then, after sliding off the bed, she padded into the other room and stood before the wooden model of the slave ship. She visualized it crammed with slaves, tossing in the ocean on its way to the West Indies. It seemed she could even see the bodies of dead slaves as they were being thrown overboard to the sharks.

Victoria covered her eyes with her hands and turned away from the model. How could this distant ancestor have sanctioned such an outrage? She shuddered.

At her next lesson, she almost pounced on Davys. "Has slavery come to an end?" she demanded.

Davys shook his head. "Oh, no. It's still practiced in the West Indies and in the United States. But, thank God, through the efforts of William Wilberforce, the Trade was abolished in 1807."

"Why don't they stop it altogether?"

"There are many reasons," Davys answered slowly, collecting his thoughts. "One significant reason is that slaves in the West Indies are earning lots of money for their owners. Another is that masters have invested heavily in the slaves."

"Well I think that all slaves should be freed," Victoria said with a firm nod of her head. "The British Government should pay the owners."

"I quite agree," Davys acknowledged with a smile. "But it will be hard to pass such legislation. Your uncle, King William, is against it. Before he was King, he visited Jamaica. On his return he proclaimed in the House of Lords that slaves are the happiest people on earth. And those who want to do away with slavery—especially Wilberforce—are fanatics."

Victoria cocked her head. "Do you know Mr. Wilberforce?"

"Of course I know him. He's an ardent evangelical Christian. He began to fight slavery in 1787 and he continued to fight it until he retired in 1825." Davys shook his head in amazement. "Thirty-eight years of fighting slavery tooth and nail. And you must keep in mind, Your Royal Highness, he has been very ill most of his life. He has been laughed at, ridiculed and defeated again and again. Yet every time he was defeated, he worked harder. Sometimes he spoke in the House of Commons for three hours at a stretch."

Victoria leaned closer to her teacher. "What was his strength?"

"Prayer. And his belief that a person should concentrate all his efforts to accomplish his project. There is nothing lukewarm about him."

Victoria felt tears beginning to push their way out. "When are they going to free the slaves that are now in bondage in the West Indies?"

"I don't know. Wilberforce has turned the crusade over to Thomas Buxton. Buxton has Quaker roots. Such people never give up. He's working on a bill to free the slaves right now. Let's pray for him."

"I certainly will," replied Victoria fervently.

John Conroy remained a malignant thorn in Victoria's side. Not only did he continue to get too familiar with her mother, but he also continued to make suggestions to Victoria about how she should live, what she should read and, especially, how she should act when she became Queen. However, in the middle of her fourteenth year, Sir John did something that softened her prejudice against him. The scheming accountant presented her mother with a spaniel named Dash.

The little dog and Victoria fell in love. Having tired of dolls, she put them away and turned her attention to Dash. And, gentle as he was, he never objected when she dressed him in the latest styles just as she had become accustomed to dressing her dolls.

That spring, Victoria's attention, like that of everyone in the United Kingdom, focused on the debates over slavery just beginning in Parliament. This time, a feeling for total abolition had seized the entire nation, even though the West Indies wailed that such legislation would ruin them.

As the debates continued, the newspapers described Wilberforce as a hero. The old slavery fighter had been ill with stomach trouble for the previous three months. Other complications also gripped him.

The bill for total abolition had been proposed by the government, and pushed by Lord Stanley, yet many still opposed it.

No one doubted the bill would pass. *But would it pass before Wilberforce received his final summons from the Lord?* Christian people throughout the United Kingdom prayed it would.

After numerous revisions, the bill, which would recompense the masters twenty million pounds for freeing their slaves, was duly prepared. On Friday, July 26, 1833, the bill had its second reading. Some worried it would not pass. Wilberforce maintained his confidence, and rightly so.

When he heard the news, the critically ill near-hunchback exclaimed, "Thank God that I should have lived to witness a day in which England is willing to give twenty million sterling for the abolition of slavery."

The survival of the bill seemed a tonic. It kept him alive throughout Saturday. But Sunday evening he began to sink. He passed away Monday morning.

On August 5, his body was laid to rest in Westminster Abbey. Both Houses of Parliament recessed that day in his honor.

Deeply moved by the accounts she read in the newspapers, Victoria had some questions for Preacher Davys. "How could Queen Elizabeth have tolerated slavery?"

"Elizabeth was a good queen," replied Davys thoughtfully. "Still, she was a victim of her times, just as David was a victim of his times. We are all victims of our times."

"Will I be a victim of my times?" Victoria glanced at him mischievously.

Davys responded seriously. "Yes, Your Royal Highness, you *will* be a victim of your times."

Victoria laughed. "My second question is this: How can I be as persistent as people like William Wilberforce?"

"There are two answers to that question. First, pray. Second, find a cause—a worthy cause—and stick with it."

After the bill abolishing slavery had been signed, Victoria went on vacation with her mother.

As usual, the Duchess insisted that she be saluted by a salvo of guns whenever she entered or left a port. This so irritated the King, he issued an order that the Duchess should never be honored with a gun salute.

His decree widened the gap between them.

Upon returning from the vacation, the Duchess became convinced that she was entitled to more rooms at Kensington. Since there were so many empty ones, she simply appropriated seventeen of them.

Horrified, Victoria asked, "Aren't you going to get permission from Uncle King?"

The Duchess lifted her haughty chin and peered at her daughter. "No. Why should I? I'm the Duchess of Kent. And you, my daughter, will be the Queen!"

Victoria started to comment, changed her mind and picked up Dash, rubbing him behind his ears. Dash responded by licking her face. Try as she might, Victoria could not keep her mind away from those seventeen rooms. Deep inside, she knew they would provide the King with yet another excuse to be angry.

On May 24, 1835, Victoria awakened with a start. It was her sixteenth birthday! As she studied her face in the mirror, she marveled that in two years she would be old enough to be Queen and reign on her own.

As she donned her robe and put on her slippers, she

thought of the coming time when she would be confirmed and receive her first communion. Thoughts of the coming ceremony caused her to wonder at her readiness in announcing to the world that she was a true Christian.

Soon after breakfast, a stream of callers came to deliver their birthday presents. The King sent a pair of sapphire earrings. His tail wagging with joy, Dash brought her a basket of barley-sugar and chocolate. Her mother's gifts included a bracelet, a shawl and a parcel of Italian books. Others brought more jewelry, a prayer book, and even a kind letter from Queen Adelaide.

As the time for Victoria's confirmation drew near, the Duchess decided the services of the Duchess of Northumberland were no longer needed to oversee the career of Victoria. This infuriated the King. He retaliated by sending word to the Archbishop of Canterbury that the confirmation not be conducted in any of the Chapels Royal. The bitter skirmish ended when Victoria's mother compromised, agreeing that it would take place in the Chapel Royal of St. James.

Victoria solemnly recorded the event in her journal:

July 30, 1835

I awoke at 7 and got up at 8. I gave Mamma a little pin and drawing done by me in recollection of today. . . . I went to St. James' Palace with the firm determination to become a true Christian, to try and comfort my Mamma in all her griefs, trials and anxieties, and to become a dutiful and affectionate daughter to her. Also to be obedient to dear Lehzen who has done so much for me. I was dressed in a white lace dress, with a white caped bonnet with a wreath of white roses around it.[4]

After the guests had been seated, King William noticed John Conroy. Glowering at him, he snapped, "We have too many in attendance. Mr. Conroy must leave."

Enraged, the Duchess stiffened and wiped her eyes. This was the most embarrassing incident in her life.

Victoria also wept. But her tears were not of rage. Rather, they were due to the solemnity of the occasion and the firm

[4]*Queen Victoria in Her Letters and Journals*, 1985, p. 14.

promises she made to the Lord.

Following a tedious sermon by the Archbishop, Victoria knelt by the side of her mother and received the wine and bread according to the rites of the Church of England. Slowly rising from her knees, she rejoiced that her very own teacher, Preacher Davys, now the Dean of Chester, had assisted during this sacred moment of consolidation in her life. She was confident he would continue to pray for her.

On the way back to Kensington, the Duchess handed Victoria a letter. "You must read this when you get home," she said. "It's *very* important." Her voice sounded unusually firm.

Alone in the room she shared with her mother, Victoria opened the envelope and scanned the letter. Then, wide-eyed, she read it again, word for word. The letter stated that since she was now a young woman, she should be more distant to Baroness Lehzen; and that she should, from then on, confide in her mother.

Dismayed, Victoria slowly folded the letter and placed it in her prayer book. Numb with anger and disappointment, she decided to share this problem with the Lord. Her mother and Lehzen were equally secure in her deepest affections. She knew she could never forsake either one. Although disappointed, she kept her chin high. For her, being a born-again believer was sufficient to keep her head high.

A few months later the trees announced fall had arrived. Victoria bid Leopold goodbye as he sailed for Belgium, then mounted her railway carriage to Ramsgate. On the way, she became quite ill. "My back aches and I feel sick in my stomach," she groaned to those around her.

Neither Conroy nor her mother felt that her illness was serious. But Lehzen was concerned. "The Princess is extremely ill," she insisted.

After a time, the Duchess believed that her daughter had more than indigestion. "Where is Doctor Clark?" she asked Conroy.

"He left for London," shrugged Conroy without moving his eyes from a herd of cattle he had been watching through the window. "But he gave me a bottle of medicine for her."

The medicine did not help. Even after Victoria crawled into her warm bed in Ramsgate she continued to worsen.

Dr. Clark returned on Friday. He looked at Victoria, unimpressed with her condition. "She'll be quite all right in a day or two," he assured her mother. Then he returned to London.

The following Wednesday, Victoria became delirious. Dr. Clark had to be persuaded to return. He became quite alarmed and gave the diagnosis that she had "bilious fever." (Modern doctors believe she had either acute tonsillitis or typhoid.)

By November, much of her hair had fallen out. She complained of her baldness and Lehzen shortened what was left, brushing it into a single puff.

During the five weeks Victoria struggled with her illness, John Conroy became alarmed that she might die. Since he knew that her death would curtail his hoped-for career, he prepared a document for her to sign. Thrusting it at her, he said, "This will indicate that you decided that when you became Queen, I was to be your private secretary." He handed her a pen.

Encouraged by the presence of Lehzen, Victoria replied, "I will not sign it." Disappointed, Conroy confronted her with several arguments. She refused to budge. "My answer is an absolute no," she repeated.

John Conroy skulked out of the room.

After being away from London for three and a half months, Victoria returned with her mother to Kensington. On the way, she kept wondering what the new seventeen-room apartment would be like. Later, she wrote:

> Our bedroom is very large and lofty and is very nicely furnished, then comes a little room for the maid and a dressing room for Mamma; then comes the old gallery which is partitioned into three large, lofty, fine and cheerful rooms. Only one of these is ready furnished; it is my sitting-room and is very prettily furnished indeed. . . . The next is my study and the last is an anteroom.[5]

---

[5]Ibid.

She expressed her one major disappointment to her mother. "Mamma, I'm over sixteen. Why do we still have to share a bedroom?"

"Because I'm your mother," replied the Duchess. Her words had the tone of finality in them.

"But, Mamma, if we have seventeen rooms, surely—"

"The answer is no."

Brokenhearted, Victoria fled to her study and picked up the newest biography of Queen Anne.

Soon Victoria had returned to her studies. Under the tutelage of Preacher Davys, she worked her way through Milton's *Paradise Lost* and Blackstone's *Commentaries on English Law*. She regretted Blackstone did not oppose the Trade of slavery. "How could that be?" she demanded after shutting the volume she had been studying.

Davys smiled. "Your Royal Highness, it's as I told you. We are all victims of our times."

During Victoria's seventeenth year, the King invited her and her mother to spend a week at Windsor Castle. The occasion was the celebration of Queen Adelaide's birthday on August 13, and his on the 21st.

As the one hundred guests filed into the elaborately decorated banquet hall on his birthday, each guest was seated at a prearranged place. The Duchess sat next to the King and her daughter opposite him. Following the dinner toast which was drunk to the King, His Majesty stood. After glaring around until there was utter silence, he began speaking in an unusually loud voice.

"I trust in God," he said angrily, "that my life may be spared for nine months longer. After which period, in the event of my death, no regency would take place. I should then have the satisfaction of leaving the royal authority to the personal exercise of that young lady," his long finger pointed at Victoria, "the Heiress presumptive of the Crown, and not in the hands of the person now near me, who is surrounded by evil advisers and who is herself incompetent to act with propriety in the station in which she would be placed. I have no hesitation in saying that I have been insulted—grossly and continually insulted—by that person, but I am determined to endure no longer a course of behavior so disrespectful of me. Amongst other things I have particularly to complain of the manner in which that young lady has been kept from my Court; she has been repeatedly kept from my drawing rooms, at which she ought always to have been present, but I am fully resolved that this shall not happen again. I would have her know that I am King and that I am determined to make my authority respected, and for the future I shall insist and command that the Princess do on all occasions appear at my Court, as it is her duty to do."[6]

When the King concluded, Victoria was in tears. Everyone else simply stared. As for the Duchess, she would have returned to Kensington immediately had it not been for the pleading of her friends.

While Victoria neared the end of her seventeenth year, the King seemed to be in remarkably good health, even though he was seventy-two and suffered from asthma. Although quite feeble, he continued to meet his appointments. On May 18, he did not rise from his chair while receiving guests. This was most unusual.

On May 24, Victoria wrote in her journal:

> Today is my 18th birthday! How old! And yet how far I am from being what I should be. I shall from this day take the firm resolution to study with renewed assiduity, to keep my attention always well fixed on whatever I'm about, and to strive to become every day less trifling and more fit for what, if Heaven wills it, I am someday to be![7]

When Victoria received word that the King's death was imminent, she was so disturbed that she skipped all her lessons except those taught by Preacher Davys. On June 15, 1837, she recorded her feelings in her journal:

> I just hear that the Doctors think my poor Uncle the King cannot last more than 48 hours! Poor man! He was always

[6]*Queen Victoria From Her Birth to the Death of the Prince Consort*, p. 129.
[7]*Queen Victoria in Her Letters and Journals*, 1985, p. 14.

kind to me, and he meant it well I know; I am grateful for it, and I shall ever remember his kindness with gratitude. He was odd, very odd and singular, but his intentions were often ill interpreted! At about ¼ p. 2. Lord Liverpool and I had a highly important conversation with him—alone.[8]

As the King's conditioned worsened, Queen Adelaide asked if he would like for her to read some prayers to him. "Oh, yes," he eagerly replied.

Fearing that he would not live until June 18, the anniversary of Waterloo, he asked the doctor to "tinker" him up so that he could enjoy that day. As the date approached, Wellington sent a messenger to enquire if he should cancel the traditional dinner that celebrated the Allied victory over Napoleon. Fumbling with a small French tricolor that had been captured in the battle, the King replied that the dinner should not be canceled, and that he hoped it might be "an agreeable one."

On June 19, Victoria mailed a letter to her Uncle Leopold.

> The King's state . . . is hopeless. . . . Poor old man! I feel sorry for him. . . . I look forward to the event which . . . is likely to occur soon, with calmness and quietness; I am not alarmed at it, and yet I do not suppose myself quite equal to all; I trust, however, that with good-will, honesty and courage I shall not . . . fail. Your advice is most excellent, and you may depend upon it I shall make full use of it.[9]

At six A.M. on Tuesday, June 20, 1837, the Duchess awakened her daughter. "The Archbishop of Canterbury and Lord Conyngham are here to see you," she said.

Victoria hurriedly donned a white dressing gown and put on slippers. Having brushed her hair, she headed for the sitting room. As she entered, both visitors sank to their knees. When she heard Conyngham say, "Queen," she extended her hand for them to kiss.

Then she listened as the Archbishop explained how he had served communion to both the King and Queen the day

---

[8]Ibid., pp. 21–22.
[9]Ibid., p. 22.

before. Victoria was delighted that he had had an easy death and that he had prepared to meet his Maker.

"His Majesty passed away at twelve past two this morning," concluded the Archbishop.

After these dignitaries had gone, Victoria dressed for breakfast. It was spine-tingling to know that since 2:12 A.M. until she had been notified, she had been the bare-foot Queen of the world's largest empire. As she sat at the table, she fervently prayed for divine help.

8
Coronation

As Victoria nibbled her first breakfast as Queen, she did not think of the food, or even of her mother sitting across from her. Deep within, she felt like a person standing by a swimming pool, hesitating to dive into the chilly water for the first time.

As Queen, she had already made two decisions she knew would displease her mother. But in her position, she decided she would do right, whether it was popular or not. She had decided, however, not to announce those decisions until later in the day. Having finished her porridge, she retired to her room in order to prepare for her private meeting with the Prime Minister, Lord Melbourne, at nine o'clock.

Victoria sat in front of the mirror as Lehzen parted her hair in the center of her forehead and swept it back over her ears in the manner of a turban. A feeling of utter inadequacy completely possessed her. Here she was, less than a month over eighteen, with no experience, barely five feet tall, weighing a mere 112 pounds, and yet assigned by providence to reign over the British Empire—the largest empire in the world. She felt as helpless as a rag doll.

"Your Majesty, you look troubled," commented Lehzen as she made finishing touches to Victoria's hair.

"I *am* troubled! Think of all the responsibility that has been thrust on me."

"That is natural at a time like this. But, Your Majesty, you must remember that God will help you just as he helped Doctor Martin Luther at Worms. I can still remember some of the trials my preacher-father had. He didn't allow them to get him down."

"What did he do?"

"He had a favorite text from the Bible. It is found in Philippians 4:13. I can still hear him quote it: 'I can do all things through Christ which strengtheneth me.' "

"I'll remember that," replied Victoria, her blue eyes lighting up.

Promptly at nine o'clock, the Queen, dressed in deep mourning, entered a private room for her conference with the Prime Minister. Seconds later, Lord Melbourne stepped inside. He was dressed in the full uniform of a Privy Councilor. Victoria greeted him and held out her hand. After he had kissed it, he said, "Since you will be meeting with the Privy Council at eleven o'clock, I thought I might be able to help you. My first question is a simple one. Would you prefer to enter the official room by yourself, or with the chief officers of the present government?"

"I will enter by myself," replied Victoria. "Also, I want you to know that you will remain Prime Minister and the other officers will also remain. You've been a good team."

Fifty-eight-year-old Lord Melbourne smiled graciously. "Your Majesty, you are very kind," he replied. Then he added, "I will now read the speech of Declaration which you will present to the Privy Council."

Victoria listened carefully as the handsome Prime Minister, now in his second term, read the short address. Her eyes on his graying sideburns and bat-winged collar surrounded by a black sash and matching tie, she remarked, "Mr. Prime Minister, I like it very much. I will do my best to read it exactly as it is written."

After Lord Melbourne had departed, Victoria read the

speech silently. Then she read it out loud. As she practiced, she realized that this statement would be the first public pronouncement she had ever made. Thoughts of the criticisms which might follow raced chills down her spine.

Eyes on the clock, the manuscript in her hand, she paced back and forth and repeated each word several times. She wanted her enunciation to be just right. Finally, at ten-thirty, she descended the narrow palace staircase to the area just outside the official room where the Privy Councilors had gathered.

Still conscious of the clock, she enunciated Melbourne's lines. Then she sat down. As the minute hand moved toward eleven o'clock, a feeling of terror swept over her. Then she remembered the text from the Bible which Lehzen had quoted. Now, as the clock ticked, she silently repeated his statement to the Philippians: "I—can—do—all—things—through—Christ—which—strengtheneth—me."

The words lifted her spirits, and lessened her fear.

Feeling better, she continued to pray until precisely eleven. At that moment, the doors opened and she made her entrance. Her uncles, Ernest, the Duke of Cumberland and Augustus, the Duke of Sussex, now approached and escorted her to the throne. As they slowly marched together, she winced at Ernest's war injuries; his eyeless socket and the livid slash across his cheek. She also became aware that Augustus had difficulty walking.

After being seated on the throne, she noticed the Prime Minister nearby on her left. This was comforting, for she knew that if she needed help, he was immediately available. Glancing at the Council, she opened the manuscript and began to read. After the first sentence, all fear left her and she finished the Declaration in a silvery voice.

Next, the swearing-in began. The Duke of Cumberland was the first to approach the throne. He knelt, kissed her hand and vowed his obeisance. Next, the Queen, realizing that it was difficult for the Duke of Sussex to move, walked over to him and extended her hand.

The swearing-in consumed a lot of time, for everyone

present was required to pledge his loyalty. Among these were the Duke of Wellington, Sir Robert Peel and Viscount Henry Palmerston.

Following the ceremonies, and after the Queen had gone, the Councilors discussed the occasion.

"I like both her modesty and firmness," commented Peel.

"She will be an agreeable change," said many who had referred to King William as "an imbecile, a profligate and a buffoon."

All the Councilors—Whig and Tory—agreed on one obvious fact: Their Queen's hand was remarkably soft!

Soon after the ceremonies at Kensington, those near St. James's Palace witnessed a historic sight. Colorfully dressed trumpeters appeared at an open window. After they had sounded their trumpets, a stentorian voice announced that Alexandrina Victoria, daughter of the Duke of Kent and granddaughter of George III, now occupied the British throne. Listeners below responded by singing *God Save the Queen*.

Many were so ecstatic that they openly wept with joy.

That occasion was the last time Victoria's double name was used. By the Queen's official command, her name was reduced to Victoria. George IV had altered her name. William IV had sought to change it. But now the Queen herself had reduced it!

Queen Victoria had a crowded schedule on this first day of her reign. One of her first acts was to gently inform her mother that she could no longer share her room. Another was to dismiss John Conroy. Dismissing him made her mother very angry. But Victoria would not rescind her order. Those who knew the situation were delighted. A wag wrote:

> Conroy goes not to Court, the reason's plain, King John
> has played his part and ceased to reign.[1]

Baroness Lehzen remained in favor. Victoria conferred upon her an original title: *Lady Attendant on the Queen*.

---

[1] *Queen Victoria, Born to Succeed*, 1964, p. 62.

She also appointed Doctor James Clark her personal physician. Melbourne helped choose the ladies who would form her household. As they considered names, he kept in mind that the Queen wanted those with a sense of humor.

The Duchess of Sutherland became the Mistress of the Robes. Others were also chosen from high-ranking circles. Altogether, she did not employ as many as Queen Anne had employed. But Victoria's choices were all similar in one way: All were dedicated Whigs. Moreover, several of them were married to members of Parliament.

Later, when the Queen and the Prime Minister were criticized for being partial to the Whigs, they merely laughed. The Tories had enjoyed similar advantages in other governments.

That twenty-first day of June did not have enough hours. Victoria rushed as she issued orders, wrote letters, had three conferences with Melbourne, one with the Archbishop of Canterbury and made plans for the next day.

That evening she dined alone. After Melbourne left at 10 P.M., she went downstairs and bid her mother good night. Then she returned to the separate room that had been prepared for her. For the first time in her life she would sleep alone.

After her evening prayers, Victoria slipped in between the cool sheets. But sleep did not come. Thoughts of the providential way in which she had come to the throne kept seeping into her mind. Then she considered the way her life had been miraculously spared from both accident and disease. There was the time when the stray bullet had gone through her sleeve. And the time as a teen when she, her mother, Lehzen and Dash had gone for a ride in a landau. While they chatted and enjoyed the clouds and soft breezes, the first horse stumbled. Its companion went down with him. As they both kicked in a frantic effort to free themselves, she feared the open, four-wheeled vehicle would overturn and kill them. Providentially, however, two gentlemen, who *just* happened to be passing by, witnessed the accident and rushed to their aid.

One of the men held the first horse's head on the ground.

This allowed Victoria and the others to escape. Next, men working together, cut the traces and freed the horses. Victoria was profoundly thankful to the gentlemen.

After reliving the incident, Victoria meditated on the reason the Lord had spared her. Within her heart she knew the answer. And that answer was as plain as the chimneys on the roof. *She had been spared because God had created her for a purpose.* Now, feeling very humble, she prayed that God would reveal that purpose and help her to be faithful in following it. Confident that God's providence still protected her, she fell asleep.

During the last week of June, workers began to move Victoria's household items to Buckingham Palace. These items included many things of sentimental value; trunks full of dolls complete with their clothing, old dresses, books she had loved as a child, a parasol, a special pair of mittens.

While wagons lumbered up to the Palace and the interior decorators prepared the Queen's apartment, she kept busy with the chores assigned to British Royalty. An examination of her journal for this period indicates some of her feelings and vast activity.

> I really have immense to do; I receive so many communications from my Ministers but I like it very much. . . . I get so many papers to sign *every* day that I have always a great deal to do; but for want of time and space I do not write these things down. I *delight* in this work. At about 10 minutes to 4 came Lord Melbourne. . . . I talked with him as usual of Political affairs, about my Household, and various other *confidential* affairs.[2]

The Queen moved into Buckingham Palace on July 13. Victoria hated to leave Kensington, the place of her birth. The vast palace had become a part of her life. Memories filled each room and Dash loved it. But the time had come and she *had* to move.

Sharing her seat with her mother in the royal coach, she started out on the historic journey to Buckingham Palace. As

---

[2]*The Youthful Queen Victoria*, 1952, p. 237.

she waved at the crowds, she also kept an eye on Dash. She hoped he would like his new home. At 2 P.M., the line of carriages reached the short avenue that led to the main entrance.

Unknown to the Queen, an old admirer had been counting the seconds as he waited for this moment. Having been a worker on the grounds, he had formed a habit of weeding the Round Pond when he knew the Princess was nearby. He did this, hoping to get a glimpse of her.

As the Queen's gilded carriage entered the gates, he quickly scrambled into his phaeton, loosed the reins and snapped the whip. The exquisitely groomed nag responded eagerly and pulled the polished wagon ahead of the cortege. Chin high, eyes straight ahead, the lowly weed-puller led the train of carriages right up to the Palace doors.

The Queen had barely set foot on the ground when Dash whizzed away. He ripped around the grounds as if competing in the Olympics. Then he stopped to inspect various items that inspired his interest. At each stop he sniffed and marked the spot in his own personal way. When Victoria eventually coaxed him to return, his tongue lolled out and his eyes shined. This, and the joy he showed when he licked her face, was warm evidence that he approved of his new home. The Queen responded by rubbing his ears.

Victoria's room was sandwiched between the bedroom of her maid and that of Lehzen. After studying the situation carefully, she placed an order. "I want an opening placed through the wall so that I can communicate instantly with the Baroness, I mean the Lady Attendant on the Queen."

"Yes, Your Majesty, I will relay your instructions immediately," replied the lord who had been showing her around.

"Thank you," replied the Queen.

The Duchess found her apartment quite separate from that of her daughter's. This annoyed her and she developed a habit of barging in on the Queen whenever she chose. Eventually, Victoria insisted that she visit only by appointment. And occasionally, her mother's note of request was returned with the words, "I'm busy," scrawled across it.

The dismissal of Conroy infuriated the Duchess more than any other problem. Through her conniving, she managed to arrange an interview for him with the Prime Minister. At that time, Conroy presented his outrageous demands for settlement. He insisted on a pension of three thousand pounds, the Grand Cross of Bath, a seat on the Privy Council, and an Irish peerage.

Incensed, Melbourne shared the demands with Victoria. They discussed the demands for several months. Finally, Victoria recommended that he be given the pension he requested, even though it was unreasonable, and be made a baron. The exorbitant payoff seemed worth it since everyone, with the exception of the Duchess, was glad to be rid of him.

During the winter months of 1837 to 1838, Victoria began to worry about her forthcoming coronation set to be celebrated on June 28. Although she had missed the coronation of Uncle William, she had vast interest in the subject. This interest increased when informed that instead of the 45,000 pounds spent on William's coronation, Parliament prepared to spend 200,000 pounds on hers.

When Queen Victoria questioned those who knew, she learned the ceremony would consist of three main parts. First, she would make a solemn oath to uphold the Protestant faith. Next would be the "unction." And finally, the actual crowning.

Not understanding all of this, she remained confident that Melbourne would insist on the necessary research and tell her precisely what to do. The crown worried her the most.

The Crown of England, St. Edward's Crown, had been designed for the coronation of Charles II. King Charles was a strong man. Standing over six feet tall, the five pound weight of the crown did not tire him. But how could she, a slender girl barely five feet tall, support it for the long period of time that would elapse while thousands of her subjects paid her homage? And the fact that each peer was not only required to kiss her hand, but to also touch the crown made the problem even more acute.

Having listened as she explained the problem, Melbourne suggested that she wear the Imperial Crown used in the coronation ceremonies of her uncles, George IV and William IV. Valid reasons, however, were advanced that the Imperial Crown was quite unsuitable. The only solution was to create a new crown.

The new Crown of State would cost one thousand pounds. Having received the approval of Her Majesty, this magnificently jeweled symbol of royalty was indeed a historic one. In addition to the finest diamonds and pearls, it featured jewels of incredible antiquity and priceless value. One of these was a sapphire allegedly taken from a ring that had been worn by Edward the Confessor. Another, the "Black Prince Ruby" had been given to the Black Prince in the fourteenth century.

The new crown pleased the Queen. It weighed only two pounds and thirteen ounces.

As summer approached and preparations for the event increased to a frantic pace, Victoria became more and more worried. Her investiture would last nearly five hours. Many intricate and important moves would be made during the ceremony. Still, no one had even mentioned rehearsal. Finally she insisted a personal rehearsal be arranged for her.

Those who witnessed the rehearsal commented that the Queen performed her part "with great grace and completeness." But Benjamin Disraeli complained that many of the participants never knew what came next.

The excitement of this extravaganza-to-come spread to the Continent. This was an opportunity for their finest young men to be exposed to the most desirable young lady in the entire world. Soon, dignitaries from all over Europe and other parts of the world converged on London. Local residents took advantage of this. One family asked and received three thousand pounds for the use of an apartment for several days.

Extremely nervous, the Queen finally went to bed on the twenty-seventh with a morbid fear that something "awful" would happen. She couldn't put out of her mind that during rehearsal it was discovered the thrones were too low and would have to be elevated. If such a major mistake could happen, how many minor mistakes would she encounter during the coronation?

She pulled the covers close around her waist, shoved the pillows behind her back and leaned into them. She took the program from her bedside stand and began to reread each line of the "unction." She believed this part to be extremely important and wanted to thoroughly understand it. By the light of her candles, she sought the meaning of each word:

> The Queen will then sit in King Edward's Chair, placed in the midst of the area over against the altar, with a faldstool before it, wherein she is to be anointed. Four Knights of the Garter hold over her a rich pall of silk or cloth of gold; the anthem being concluded, the Dean of Westminster, taking the ampulla and spoon from off the altar, holdeth them ready, pouring some of the holy oil into the spoon, and with it the Archbishop anointeth the Queen in the form of a cross on the crown of the head and on the palms of both hands, saying, "Be thou anointed with holy oil, as kings, priests, and prophets were anointed."[3]

Considering the meaning of this procedure, the Queen prayed that it might not be a mere formality; but that it would inspire—and dominate—each second of her reign.

Following a fitful night of twisting and turning, the sound of cannon fire in the park awakened her. The repeated salvos announced to the world what she had not been able to eradicate from her mind. The day had come—Thursday, June 28, 1838—the day of her coronation as the Queen of the world's largest empire.

Victoria turned over in bed. Opening bleary eyes to the clock, she groaned when she noticed it was only 4 A.M. Wearily, she adjusted the pillow and closed her eyes. But the sound of bands and crowds continued to seep into her room, making it impossible to sleep. Forcing herself, she remained in bed until 7 A.M.

Victoria faced breakfast without appetite. Following two

---

[3]*Westminster Abbey*, 1891, p. 86.

attempts, she managed to swallow some porridge. Her half sister, Princess Feodora, visited with her in her room until it was time for her to be dressed.

On this morning, the hairdresser had an especially precise task. Her hair had to be combed in such a way that her forehead would be exposed for the anointing and so that the crown would remain secure. The hairdresser parted her hair in the center, twisted each side into a long braid, then fastened them into a bun on the back top of her head. Next, as she noted in her journal, she dressed in her "House of Lords costume."

Clad in white, accompanied by the Duchess of Sutherland, Mistress of Robes, and Lord Albemarle, Master of the Horse, the Queen stepped into the Royal coach and headed toward the Abbey. A gold circlet, brilliant with diamonds, glistened on her head. The coachman flicked his whip at 10 A.M.

As the carriage wheels began to turn, cannon fire signaled the Queen was on her way. Dense crowds lined the streets, slowing the progress of the carriage. Victoria waved to everyone.

> I reached the Abbey amid deafening cheers at a little after half-past eleven; I first went into the robing-room quite close to the entrance where I found my eight train-bearers . . . all dressed alike and beautifully in white satin and silver tissue with wreaths of corn-ears in front, and a small one of pink roses around the plait behind, and pink roses in the trimming of the dresses.
>
> After putting on my mantle, and the young ladies having properly got hold of it and Lord Conygham holding the end of it, I left the robing-room . . .[4]

Prime Minister Melbourne carried the Sword of State, followed by the Bishops with the Chalice, the Patena and the Bible in their jeweled hands. Victoria paused a moment, then started down the long aisle. This ancient building held ten thousand of Britain's most celebrated notables, along with the distinguished guests from other nations. They filled every

---

[4]*Queen Victoria in Her Letters and Journals*, 1985, p. 34.

space, crowding with the memories of all the British sovereigns crowned there (except Edward V) since the death of William the Conqueror. Overwhelmed, the Queen paused, clasped her hands and caught her breath. She felt herself pale at the unbelievable splendor.

Peers crowded the seats on one side of the aisle while peeresses crowded the seats on the other side. Diamonds, thousands of diamonds, together with other jewels winked as sunshine squeezed through the colored windows.

In addition to seas of diamonds, there were coronets—tiny crowns sprinkled with diamonds and other jewels. The owners kept them on cushions or held them in their hands in readiness to place on their heads at the sublime moment.

As Victoria slowly pressed forward, she became conscious that her train-bearers were having trouble. Their trains had been improperly designed so their feet tended to catch in their gowns. Each trip jerked the Queen's train. Ignoring the problem, Victoria kept her chin up and her eyes forward as she advanced toward the high altar.

The tension increased as Victoria neared the place where she would kneel. Lifting her eyes, she watched Melbourne moving ahead. The sight of him encouraged her. After the final step, the boys of Westminster School cried in one voice, "Vivat Victoria Regina!" The Archbishop then affirmed that Victoria was "the undoubted Queen of this realm."

A spontaneous shout from the crowd answered his declaration, "God save Queen Victoria." The Queen then turned north, south and west as the customary Litany was recited. Next, she made her oath that as Queen and Defender of the Faith, she would uphold the Protestant Faith which had been "established by law."

Following her oath, she knelt while the choir sang, "Veni, Creator Spiritus." As she lingered on her knees with her head bowed and hands clasped, the choir boys began to sing, *Come, Holy Ghost, Our Souls Inspire*. As she listened, she forgot about the gold brocade hanging from her shoulders, the sea of diamonds and even the presence of Melbourne. One thought dominated her mind. *Oh God, provide me with the guidance I will need during every moment of my reign.*

Following this holy moment, Victoria quietly stood and entered St. Edward's Chapel, immediately behind the high altar. There, she removed her robe and kirtle (long gown) and put on the supertunica of gold cloth, also in the shape of a kirtle. This was put over a singular sort of linen gown trimmed with lace. She also took off her circlet of diamonds, then proceeded bareheaded into the Abbey.

As the Queen advanced toward the Coronation Chair, the train-bearers accompanied her. While seated, the four Knights of the Garter held the cloth of gold over her head. Then the Archbishop anointed her with "holy" oil. He made a cross on her forehead and touched each of her hands with an additional drop.

After the anointing, the Dalmatic robe, lined with ermine and sewn out of gold cloth was brought forward. This overgarment, made with wide slits for her arms, was then placed over her supertunica. Here, the Archbishop attempted to present her with the orb, unaware it had already been placed in her hand. Then she was handed the scepter. As she held it, the Archbishop placed the ring on her finger. Unfortunately, he pushed it onto the wrong finger and she almost screamed with pain. (Later, she soaked her hand in ice water in order to remove it.)

A tomb-like silence settled over the audience. Each knew the awaited climax was at hand. Edging their seats and clutching their coronets, all were tense as seconds split into fragments and fragments split into even more fragments. Eyes riveted forward as they watched the acting Dean of Westminster hand the crown to the magnificently robed Archbishop.

From her place just above the Royal Box, Lehzen watched every move—especially those of the young Queen whom she had endeavored to shape since her childhood.

Solemnly, the Archbishop placed the crown on Queen Victoria's head. At that precise moment, a shaft of pure sunlight streamed through an upper window and illuminated both her face and the crown. Each of the nearly three thousand one hundred jewels responded by blazing with an almost heavenly light.[5]

Suddenly, every coronet perched on its owner's head. It was like hundreds of thousands of fireflies flashing at the same time. Simultaneously, cannons in all the parks roared their salutes. And as they roared, trumpets blared and drums beat. And at that moment, the crowd stood and shouted as one voice: "God save the Queen. God save the Queen."

Crowned, Victoria remained on her throne while her subjects came forward to pay their homage. As she waited for the first one, she glanced at the balcony. She caught Lehzen's eyes and both exchanged smiles—smiles neither would forget.

Soon there was a long line of peers, waiting their turns to kneel at her feet, kiss her hand and touch her crown. In the midst of the line, Lord Rolle, a decrepit eighty-seven-year-old gentleman slowly worked himself forward with the help of two other peers. He had just reached the Queen's stool when he stumbled and rolled to the bottom of the steps. There he remained, all tangled in his robes. Others helped him to his feet. Bravely, he tried again to get to the Queen. Crippled as he was, this was impossible. Alarmed, the Queen rose, went to him and extended her hand.

The Queen's Christlike action touched off more enthusiasm than the old Abbey had ever known. It all but exploded with wave after wave of ecstatic joy. Everyone—heads of state, ambassadors, peers and peeresses—leaped to their feet. The windows shook with their loud cheers. Eyes overflowed. Thousands shouted, "God bless her!"

After the last one had rendered homage, Victoria left her throne, removed her crown and took the Sacrament. Then, she replaced the crown and returned to her throne. The ceremony completed, the Queen stood to leave. The organ burst forth with the Hallelujah Chorus. The accompanying choir sang their best. Again, there were swimming eyes. For the

---

[5]The crown contained 2,783 diamonds, 277 pearls, 17 sapphires, 11 emeralds and 5 rubies.

words, *King of kings and Lord of lords*, seemed most appropriate for this significant turn in British history.

Victoria felt extremely tired when she headed toward Buckingham Place. Although her finger was still swollen from the misplaced ring, she waved at all the crowds. Back at home, she sank into a chair, kicked off her shoes and ordered a cup of tea.

It had been a hard day.

9

Royal Frustrations

As one of her daily sessions with Prime Minister Melbourne neared the end, Queen Victoria had a question. "I've been puzzled about the size of the British Empire. How large is it?"

"Your Majesty, that is hard to answer. You must understand that we do not have identical control over each colony. Some, not all, are *Crown Colonies*. Crown Colonies are ruled by Great Britain. You, as Queen, will be appointing their governor-generals."

Victoria lifted her brows. "That's a lot of responsibility!"

"Don't worry. The actual selection will be made by those assigned to that task. You will make the announcement and sign the legal papers. Your task is a mere formality."

"Then I'm only a figurehead?"

"Your Majesty, you are not just a figurehead. You are a *needed* figurehead."

Victoria searched his face. "What do you mean?"

"For a while, the United Kingdom thought it could get along without a king or queen, and so they allowed Oliver Cromwell to get into power. Cromwell ruled as the Lord Protector. After his death, he was followed by his son Richard. But the people soon tired of this form of government. Like the Israelites in the Old Testament, they wanted a king. And so in 1660, Charles II, the son of Charles I who had been executed by Cromwell, was acclaimed king.

"Thus, the British Empire reaffirmed the monarchy. Even so, we have some colonies, such as Malta that are self-governing yet owe allegiance to the British Crown. We also have protectorates—"

"How about India?"

"Ah, that's a strange situation. Right now, India is ruled by the British East India Company. This company has the cooperation of British troops."

"But doesn't Britain appoint the governor-general of India?"

"Yes, yes, of course. After Lord Cornwallis surrendered to George Washington at Yorktown, he was made the governor-general of India. He remained under the shadow of the British East India Company." The Prime Minister rubbed his brow. "I wouldn't be surprised if we had full control of India in a few years. Many people are unhappy about the harsh measures of that company. I'm afraid they've been exploiting the people. Exploitation is not the British system. If George III had been more generous with the American colonies, we would not have lost them."

Victoria sighed. "It's all very interesting. But, Mr. Prime Minister, you haven't yet told me the size of the British Empire."

"There's no way to be absolutely certain about that. I've heard estimates that one fourth of the people on this planet extend their allegiance to the British Crown." He smiled. "Your Majesty, you have a lot of subjects!"

Victoria laughed a little uneasily. "I do have a lot of responsibility. But how can I help all those people if I have no power?"

"By your influence."

Victoria tipped her head to one side. "My influence?"

"Yes, your influence. You've already used it."

Victoria leaned forward. "How?"

"Do you remember how you helped Lord Rolle at your coronation?"

"Certainly. That was nothing. The old man needed help . . ."

The Prime Minister smiled broadly. "True. Yet the whole United Kingdom is talking about it. They say you've brought in a new era! You must keep in mind that your every action is watched. When you do a noble thing, it has a domino effect and motivates others. Right now, Your Majesty, you are the most popular person in the entire British Empire. You can influence everyone for good."

A pensive look crossed Victoria's face. "I hope so."

"And so do I. Solomon said, 'Righteousness exalteth a nation: but sin is a reproach to any people.' "

She bowed her head. "Be frank with me, Mr. Prime Minister, will my popularity last?"

Melbourne laughed. "It will go up and it will come down. Human beings are fickle. Governments come and go. A person may be loved one day and hated the next. You are, Your Majesty, sitting on a throne with a Damocles sword suspended over your head by one hair. But whereas I may be voted out of office by Parliament, you will remain Queen for the rest of your life. Even so, you must depend upon the Lord."

"Of that, I'm sure," agreed Victoria. A sour look crossed her face. "I want you to tell me why I'm not queen of Hanover. Both my uncles, George and William were their kings. Should I not be their queen?"

"Your Majesty, you are not their queen because their constitution forbids a woman to ever sit on the throne."

"So?"

"Your uncle, the Duke of Cumberland will be their king."

"Maybe that's a good thing." Victoria laughed.

"It's not only good, it's providential," agreed Melbourne, joining in her laughter.

Although she had been coronated, Victoria's life continued in much the same manner as it had since King William had passed away.

Victoria's day started about 8 A.M. After a breakfast in her own room, she read all the dispatches. These included briefs about most items of importance. She also transacted business at this time. This business included making suggestions and signing documents. At eleven or twelve, Prime Minister Melbourne usually consulted with her for up to an hour. With him she discussed important bills, news from the colonies and any major problem that had arisen.

At about two o'clock, she along with numerous others, mounted horses and spent two hours riding—often at full gallop. The Queen preferred large horses and rode sidesaddle. She always arranged for Melbourne to ride on her left and for an equerry to ride on her right.

Following this riding period, Victoria spent the rest of the afternoon engaged in various forms of recreation. If her guests had children, she enjoyed romping with them. She also had a taste for music. This included singing. Likewise, she enjoyed books. Biographies of her ancestors were among her favorites.

One guest, Sallie Coles Stevenson, wife of the American Ambassador, described a dinner she had with the Queen:

> At seven P.M. I was dressed all to my white crape hat with ostrich feathers, which had not arrived from the milliners— black silk, with black crape over it, trimmed with crape and black rosettes of berries and leaves, jet ornaments, necklace, earrings, bracelets; & at five minutes to the time we arrived. And we did not get to the palace until many minutes after the precisely (sic) had passed.
>
> In trepidation I ran up the grand & magnificent staircase with as fleet a step as was consistent with my dignity, and through the superb suite of apartments until we reached the grand receiving room, where all the company were assembled, standing waiting for the appearance of her Majesty. In a short time the glass doors of the next apartment opened, & she came forth in deep black, attended by all her ladies-in-waiting, maids-of-honor, & her "august" mother (the newspaper language), with her attendants, a goodly train. As we stood in a circle, the little Queen approached us & said something to each person with a calm and gentle dignity, as perfectly self-possessed as if we had all been statues. Her mother followed, repeating the same ceremonious courtesy, & then dinner was announced. She [the Queen] took the arm

of Count Pozzo di Borgo (the Russian Ambassador) & led the way.

The folding-doors flew open. The band which was stationed in the marquee below, struck up and we found ourselves in a magnificent banqueting-room, brilliantly lighted, and the table covered with a service of gold so splendid it dazzled one's eyes to look upon it. The Queen sat midway the (sic) table, with her lords-in-waiting at each end. Her little Majesty eat (sic) with a good appetite, and did full justice to the rich viands. After the second course, the lord-in-waiting who had led me to dinner rose and drank to the Queen's health. All stood up but the Queen.

When the dinner was over, her Majesty rose and passed out first. We followed through the rich and gorgeous apartments, which reminded me of the descriptions in the Arabian Nights, until she reached the grand drawing room, when she paused and a circle formed around her. No one must speak first to her Majesty . . .[1]

Drawing room etiquette was always extremely formal. There, no one but the Queen was allowed to begin or change a conversation. On one evening, the Queen approached a guest. "Have you been riding today, Mr. Greville?" inquired the Queen.

"No madam, I have not," he replied.

"It was a fine day."

"Yes, madam, a very fine day."

"It was rather cold, though," commented the Queen.

"It was rather cold, madam," agreed Greville.

"Your sister, Lady Francis Egerton, rides, I think, doesn't she?"

"She does ride sometimes, madam."

At this juncture, ever-courageous Greville took the lead. "Has Your Majesty been riding today?"

"Oh yes, a very long ride."

"Has Your Majesty got a nice horse?"

"Oh, a very nice horse."[2] Having said this, she smiled and nodded. Greville understood the signal and automatically bowed and she turned to the next person.

---

[1] *Victoria & Albert and Mrs. Stevenson*, 1957, pp. 82–83.
[2] *Queen Victoria*, 1921, pp. 97–98.

After the guests had retired, Melbourne frequently lingered for an hour or two. Again, the subject was business. Politics. Appointments. Legislation. At the conclusion of this conference, which often lasted until eleven, Melbourne excused himself and Victoria returned to her room. There, she sometimes relaxed by giving Dash an evening bath before she retired.

At first, this routine was exciting. Soon, it became a bore. In time, being robed, unrobed, forcing herself to smile and constantly hold out her hand to be kissed, became a duty rather than a pleasure. At the close of one monumental occasion, she lamented to her diary that her hand had been "kissed three thousand times."

This form of exciting schedule, however, was soon clouded by a crisis. This crisis so thoroughly upset her that she frequently cried herself to sleep.

Lord Melbourne was in political trouble!

The Tories had, for a long time, sought an excuse to upset the Whig Government of Lord Melbourne. Soon, an ideal scandal to exploit dropped into their midst. This scandal centered on Lady Flora Hastings, a Maid of Honor employed by the Duchess of Kent.

To many, it seemed that this unmarried woman was expecting. Each month her abdomen was a little larger than the previous month. Alarmed by the gossip, the Queen inquired into the problem. To her dismay, she learned that both her own doctor, Sir James Clarke and the Court Ladies were agreed that Lady Hastings had fallen into sin. Incensed, the Queen noted in her diary: "We have no doubt that she is—to use plain words—with child!"

Deeply troubled, Victoria discussed the matter with Lord Melbourne. "What shall we do?" she demanded.

"Let's just wait and see what happens," he replied.

While the Queen and the Ladies waited, Lady Hastings continued to expand. As she expanded, so did the gossip. Each day, Victoria became more furious. She had determined that her court would be a virtuous one. A sarcastic note in her diary indicates how she felt: "Mama is here with her amiable and virtuous lady!"

Finally, when the gossipers became too shrill and raised their eyebrows too high, it was decided that Doctor Clarke should examine Lady Hastings and determine the truth. The truth was that her swelling had been due to other causes— and that she was still a virtuous woman!

Lady Hasting's brother was extremely disturbed. (Several months later, his anger turned into rage, when his sister died and the postmortem examination indicated that she had been suffering from a growth in her liver.)

Red-faced and determined, Lord Hastings confronted Melbourne and demanded that Doctor Clarke be dismissed. Caught in a dilemma, for some were whispering behind their hands that the Queen had originated the gossip, Melbourne sent him a rather abrupt letter in which he insisted the case was closed.

Prime Minister Melbourne might have survived that crisis had it not been that a far more serious crisis brewed in Canada. In Lower Canada, the French Catholics were frustrated at being ruled by overseas British Protestants. Their rebellion soon spread to Upper Canada. These minor rebellions so upset the British Government, they sent a representative to Canada to study the matter. Britain had lost the American colonies and they didn't want to lose Canada.

Soon, it became apparent that due to this colonial problem, the Melbourne Government could not last. After surviving by a margin of only five votes in the House of Commons, Melbourne called on the Queen and suggested that she summon the Duke of Wellington for a conference.

Fearing she would never see Melbourne again, Victoria wept. During this tempestuous time, she described her feelings quite frankly in her diary under the date May 8, 1839. "I sobbed much again and kept holding his hand for sometime fast in one of mine, as if I felt in doing so he could not leave me. . . . He then got up, and we shook hands again and he kissed my hand, I crying dreadfully."[3]

---

[3]*Queen Victoria in Her Letters and Journals*, 1985, p. 46.

Victoria had secret hopes the Duke of Wellington would be willing to head a Tory Government. The victor of Waterloo, however, refused. His excuse was his growing deafness. The Duke suggested she summon Sir Robert Peel. She winced at this. He was not one of her favorite characters. But she had no alternative.

The next day, Peel called on the Queen a little after two in the afternoon. The tall, well-dressed man, obviously ill at ease, occasionally glanced at his toe while she asked him to form a new Tory Government. At the conclusion of her request, Peel asked, "Your Majesty, are you willing to give up your ladies?"

Thoroughly alarmed, Victoria tried to remain calm. "How many?"

"All of them."

"Why?"

"Because, Your Majesty, they are Whigs."

"So?"

"Many of their husbands are members of Parliament."

"So?"

"They are Whigs and the Whigs are my opponents."

As Victoria thought about her Lady of the Bedchamber, the Lady of the Robes and the Maids of Honor, her gorge began to rise. These women had been efficient and she did not want to give them up. Finally, forcing a smile, she replied, "I am sorry. I will not give them up."

This disturbed Peel. But he refused to surrender to a mere nineteen-year-old girl, who by chance, happened to be Queen.

On May 10, he wrote her a long diplomatic letter in which he laid out his position.

Victoria refused to submit. "My household ladies will remain," she said, pushing out her diminutive chin to its utmost limit. She then sent a letter to Melbourne in which she expressed her wish that he dine with her the following Sunday.

Melbourne was delighted.

On Sunday, as she rode to church, a throng of well-wishers greeted her, shouting, "Bravo!" and "The Queen forever!"

While Melbourne and the Queen dined, he felt his optimistic best, sounding off with some of his most cherished bits of wisdom.

After dinner, Melbourne remarked, "Your Majesty, I'm afraid that I must leave, for I have an appointment at ten o'clock." He kissed her hand and smiled. "I don't want to be late."

Thoroughly put out, Sir Robert Peel called on the Queen and informed her that since she refused to dismiss her ladies, he found it impossible to launch a Tory Government.

On the following morning, while the Whig Cabinet met, Melbourne showed them the various dispatches he had from the Queen and others concerning the dismissal of the Household Ladies. The ecstatic cabinet vowed they would not forsake such a woman. The conclusion of the fracas saw the Whigs remain in power and Lord Melbourne remain Prime Minister.

That evening, the Queen celebrated by having a ball at the palace. Both the Duke of Wellington and Sir Robert attended, but neither was quite himself.

The Queen did not get to bed until 4 A.M. As she relaxed, a warm feeling of satisfaction swept over her. Melbourne had been a real friend. He had stood by her and helped her many times. Now he was back. Wonderful!

Victoria and Melbourne did not always agree. While he contended the right of a man to have an affair or two, she believed in absolute chastity. Melbourne also disagreed with her about drinking wine to excess. Her conflict with him had arisen over the men's custom of staying in the dining room after the women had gone, then draining far too many bottles of wine. As the Queen in her own palace, she had put a stop to this. Melbourne had been quite unhappy about her actions. Nonetheless, her decrees had minimized drunkenness in Buckingham Palace.

Queen Victoria's popularity, however, did not remain at

the peak. When she stepped onto the balcony at Ascot and joined Melbourne, a voice jeered, "Mrs. Melbourne!" And later, when she drove away, several hissed at her. It unnerved her, and she exclaimed, "Those abominable women ought to be flogged!"

After she had cooled from this shock, Victoria discussed the problem with Melbourne. "It's as I told you," he replied, "a person's popularity will go up, and it will come down."

"And you were right," agreed Victoria, forcing a smile.

10
Romance!

Just as she had tired of her more than one hundred dolls, Victoria wearied of all the formality she had to endure. At first she enjoyed having ladies curtsy and gentlemen bow as they murmured, "Your Majesty." But now, having to listen to those dreadful words scores of time each day and to see them in every letter was a pain. Often, in her private moments, she wished she knew someone who could speak without bowing and could address her with a pet name.

It would be wonderful to hear someone say, "Drina, let's go for a walk." Or, "Vickelchen, I just love your hairdo." It would also be a pleasure to have a friend who could turn around and walk out of the room without backing out.

But she was not allowed these common pleasures for only one reason—she was the Queen of the British Empire.

Late in the spring, Victoria opened her heart to Lord Melbourne. When she finished, her eyes brimmed with tears.

The Prime Minister listened patiently, then smiled. "Your Majesty, your problem has an extremely simple solution."

"It does?"

"Yes, quite simple. It's a solution that could be very pleasant."

Victoria leaned forward with anticipation. "Tell me quick. What is it?"

"Your Majesty," Lord Melbourne said, walking across the room toward her, "you ought to get married!"

"Get married?" she replied in disbelief.

"Yes, get married. Marriage would solve two problems. A good husband would make you happy and the two of you could supply some needed heirs to the throne. It would be wonderful if you could bring into the world a prince or princess of Wales. Such a person would give the United Kingdom some real security."

"Queen Anne had seventeen children, but they all died." Victoria frowned. "And her husband George of Denmark was rather useless."

"True. Still, *you* should get married." Melbourne smiled.

Victoria remained silent with her thoughts for a long time. Then she said, "Mr. Prime Minister, marriage is not easy for those who have royal blood."

"Why not?"

"Because we're not supposed to marry commoners. We're supposed to marry someone else with royal blood and if possible, to marry someone who will improve the political situation." Victoria stopped suddenly and bit her lip.

"And so?" Melbourne encouraged.

"Three years ago, King William got it into his head that I should marry a son of the Prince of Orange. And to further his plan, he invited the Prince and his two sons to visit him. This caused a complication, for Mamma had already invited her brother Ernest and his two sons—Prince Ernest and Prince Albert—to visit us at Kensington.

"When Uncle William heard about this, he almost blew apart. This was because he hated everyone from Coberg, especially my mother, Leopold and the Duke. In his rage, he ordered the Foreign Secretary to inform my mother that she should not invite her brother nor her nephews to England.

"But Mamma can be so stubborn. Since King William could not stop them, he ordered they should be received with due military honors." Victoria sighed. "Do you know what that uncle of mine did? He sent word that they should be lodged in a hotel!"

Victoria let a sly smile play on her lips. "Again my mother was stubborn. All three of them stayed with us at Kensington."

Lord Melbourne looked amused. "And what happened to the Prince of Orange and his sons?"

"The King and Queen Adelaide threw a ball for them at St. James's Palace."

"Did you see any of them?"

Victoria did a small turn, smiling in memory. "I saw all of them and we all had a good time together."

"And which of the four princes do you prefer?"

"Albert, of course. He's smarter, better looking and kinder than any of them. He's almost perfect." She hesitated. "But Mr. Prime Minister, what am I to do? Since I'm the Queen, no man would be permitted to propose to me."

"Again, the solution is simple. Your Majesty, if you're interested in one of them, you should propose to him."

Victoria blushed. "P-p-propose t-t-to h-h-him?"

"Certainly. Why not?"

Victoria turned away from Melbourne's piercing stare. "I'll have to think about it."

One evening, after signing hundreds of documents, Victoria could not keep her thoughts away from Albert. Eventually, curious about what she might have confided to her journal about him three years before, she flipped back to June 10, 1836. Laughing to herself, she read:

> At nine we all breakfasted for the last time together! It was our last happy happy breakfast with this dear Uncle and these dearest beloved Cousins whom I do love so very, very dearly, much more dearly than any other Cousins in the world. Dearly as I love Ferdinand and also good Augustus [sons of Uncle Ferdinand, Duke of Saxe-Coburg], I love Ernest and Albert more than them, oh yes, MUCH more. Augustus was like a good affectionate child, quite unacquainted with the world, phlegmatic, and talking but very little; but dearest Ernest and dearest Albert are so grown up in their manners . . . and are very clever, particularly Albert who is the most reflecting of the two. . . . Albert used always to have some fun and some clever witty answer at breakfast

and everywhere; he used to play and fondle Dash so funnily too. Both he and Ernest are extremely attentive to whatever they hear and see. . . .

After closing the journal, Victoria searched her heart. As she did so, each of these cousins, along with other would-be suitors who had been called to her attention by the match-makers, paused in front of her. She studied each one in the manner of a connoisseur in a fine art gallery. Albert undoubt-edly qualified as the most handsome in the entire group. He was also the most learned, kindest and the most considerate. She loved his curly, light-brown hair, pencil-size moustache and thin sideburns that dropped straight down from his hair to the back of his jaw, thus framing his clean-shaven, well-molded chin.

Victoria thought about getting lost in his intense blue eyes. Then, thinking about how she'd have to stand on tiptoe in order to kiss him, she laughed.

After her evening prayers, she crawled into bed. But she could not sleep. *What if she were too fat? Or, horrors, what would she do if he did not want her?*

Candle in hand, she weighed herself. She shuddered at the figure. The needle stopped at 114 pounds. Terrible! Next, she studied herself in the mirror and debated on whether or not she should change her hairstyle. *Should she braid it and coil it on top of her head like a spring, or should she retain the style she had worn at her coronation?*

Back under the sheets, she became more realistic. *How could she propose to Albert? Should she do it by mail or in person? What kind of language should she use? Should she approach Melbourne and ask his advice?*

While pondering these questions, Victoria thought of the meetings and papers she must sign the next day and closed her eyes. She *had* to get to sleep.

In the fragments of time between heavy appointments, Victoria pondered over the heartbreaks she would have to endure if she married the wrong man. Her grandfather, George III, had had his bride selected for him. Neither he nor she had seen the other until the day of their wedding. Even so, Grandfather George and Grandmother Charlotte had enjoyed a long and happy marriage.

Her uncles on her father's side had not fared so well. Most had and were enduring one heartbreak after another. Determined that such catastrophes would not happen to her, she decided to pray about the matter—and do some investigating.

Although Victoria had often heard her mother speak of her brothers and sisters, the only one she had really thought about was her favorite, Uncle Leopold, King of the Belgians. Now, she began to dig into the genealogy of this family where a brother had fathered both Ernest and Albert. *What kind of man was Albert's father and what kind of woman was his wife?*

Without much effort, Victoria learned that while serving as Coburg's reigning Duke, Ernest married Princess Louise of Saxe-Gotha-Altenburg. He was thirty-three and she was seventeen. Within weeks, Louise discovered that her new husband was both a drunk and a woman-chaser.

Their first child, Ernest, was born in 1818.

The next part of the story frightened Victoria. It had been gossiped that at this point Louise had been indiscreet—that Albert had been fathered by a secret lover. In addition, the lover was half-Jewish!

Suddenly Victoria's world was in a whirl. *Could it be that Albert—her perfect Albert—was illegitimate? And if she should marry him, would her children be considered illegitimate and be barred from the throne in the same manner in which King William's ten children were barred from the throne?*

The whole idea was utterly devastating.

After several sleepless nights, Victoria decided to do some more investigation. During her research, she discovered that after his wife's death in 1817, Leopold had spent the following year with the Duke and Louise in Coburg. Since Albert was born on August 26, 1819, any indiscretion would have to have been committed in the latter part of 1818. This being true, would it be reasonable to assume that Louise would have been brazen enough to have carried on an affair with a distinguished lover while Uncle Leopold lived in the same house? Victoria didn't think so.

Three other facts encouraged Victoria to believe the ugly stories she heard could only be rumors. 1. It was quite obvious Louise favored Albert. 2. Uncle Leopold favored her contemplated marriage to his nephew Albert. 3. Several years after Albert's birth, Louise left the Duke. After a divorce, she married a lieutenant.

Best of all, everyone around her—including her mother, the Duke's sister—favored the marriage.

Having made up her mind to know Albert better, Victoria made arrangements for him to come to London to visit her. One hour with him and she made up her mind. The warmth of his handclasp when he told her good night assured her she had won his heart.

The next morning, October 15th, she sent a messenger to him requesting he call on her for a private interview.

They sat together on a plain sofa pushed against the wall. Clothed in a white gown that reached the floor, Victoria sat on Albert's right, her hair parted in the center and coiled in a bun at the back of her head.

Albert was dressed in a long formal coat and cream-colored trousers. A stovepipe hat in his hand indicated his readiness to leave the moment she gave the signal.

Victoria later wrote in her journal:

> I said to him that I thought he must be aware why I wished him to come here, and that would make me too happy if he would consent to what I wished (to marry me); we embraced each other over and over again, and he was so kind, so affectionate; Oh! to feel I was, and am, loved by such an Angel as Albert was too great delight to describe! He is perfection; perfection in every way—in beauty—in everything! I told him I was quite unworthy of him and kissed his dear hand—he said he would be very happy "das Leben mit dir zu zubringen" [to share his life with you] and was so kind and seemed so happy, that I really felt it was the happiest moment of my life, which made up for all I had suffered.

> Oh! how I adore and love him, I cannot say!! How I will strive to make him feel as little as possible the great sacrifice he has made; [I told him it was a great sacrifice]—which he wouldn't allow. . . . I feel that happiest of human beings.[1]

Albert responded to that meeting with Victoria by writing her a letter.

> Dearest, greatly beloved Victoria—How is it that I have deserved so much love, so much affection? I cannot get used to the reality of all that I see and hear, and have to believe that Heaven has sent me an angel whose brightness shall illumine my life . . . In body and soul your slave, your loyal, ALBERT.[2]

Now engaged to be married, Queen Victoria faced two formidable tasks. Both frightened her. First, she must face the Privy Council and inform them of her intentions. Second, she must negotiate with Parliament in regard to Albert's rank, duties and income.

Dreading both tasks, she began to prepare herself by consulting with Melbourne, studying similar situations that had arisen and by making her problems a matter of earnest prayer.

[1]*Queen Victoria from Her Birth to the Death of Prince Consort*, p. 187.
[2]*Victoria and Albert*, 1977, p. 142.

11
Storms

W hile Victoria and Albert prepared for their wedding, both realized there would be storms ahead; but neither realized the intense severity of those storms.

November 1839 brought cold weather to London. Even though the heating in Buckingham Palace proved defective, the temperature did not concern Victoria. Her first priority was to decide on the rank and title that should be awarded Albert. King Leopold had written that he should be made a peer. Melbourne objected to this. He said a peerage would automatically put Albert in the House of Lords. That would inspire many to accuse him of seeking to interfere in British politics.

Victoria also scorned a peerage, but for a different reason. "A peerage isn't good enough for Albert," she informed Melbourne. "He should be made King Consort!"

"Your Majesty, I cannot agree with that," Melbourne replied. "I think the fact that he will be your husband is high enough rank for him at the moment."

This unexpected barricade made Victoria unhappy. Yet she inwardly smiled, knowing the sublime honor she could confer upon him without consulting anyone. She decided to do just that after she had endured the horror of meeting with the Privy Council.

On November 23, eighty-two members of that powerful group crowded into the regular chamber at Buckingham Palace.

While awaiting the precise moment to step through the doors and face the group, Victoria rehearsed the speech Lord Melbourne had written for her.

"Are you frightened?" asked her lady.

Victoria managed a smile. "Of course I am. But I faced a far more terrifying moment a while back."

"When was that?"

"On October 15, when I proposed to Albert. Having survived that, I feel I can do anything." Victoria stood a little taller and smoothed her dress. "Yes, anything!"

Suddenly, the folding doors parted and she stepped inside. In preparing for the occasion, she had had a tiny framed photograph of Albert attached to her bracelet. With this bracelet on her wrist, she felt Albert's presence and with that presence, a strength and peace.

As the sea of counselors waited with anticipation, she felt even more nervous than on that dreadful occasion when she read her first speech to them as Queen.

Hands shaking, Victoria found it difficult to read the document which had been written on thin paper. It crackled as she struggled to hold it steady. With concentrated effort, she just managed to keep a quiver out of her voice.

At the conclusion of the speech, several congratulated her on her fine composure.

In the speech, Melbourne had neglected to mention that Albert was Protestant. The newspapers pounced on this omission, which sent the country into turmoil. This was a divisive issue, for some of the Coburgs had converted to Catholicism, and Albert had made a trip to Rome. All of this aggravated Victoria since she knew that Albert was not only a Lutheran but an intense admirer of Martin Luther.

The ordeal with the Privy Council over, a jubilant Victoria dashed off a letter to Albert. Her moment to bestow the sublime honor upon him was at hand. She informed him that she had made him a member of the Most Noble Order of the

Garter. On December 7th, he replied:

> It gives me great pleasure that you intend soon to send
> me the Garter. I should like to have the uniform also, as I
> think it very essential to try it on and have it fitted here, so
> that when I come to England I am not made ridiculous by a
> badly fitting uniform as I was the last time owing to having
> the wrong kind of hat.[1]

Victoria *assumed* that Parliament would vote Albert an
income of fifty thousand pounds—the same amount which
they had paid Leopold when he married Charlotte and Queen
Anne's Consort, George of Denmark.

One member of Parliament, gloomy about current financial conditions, moved that Albert's income be set at twenty-
one thousand pounds. A large vote rejected his suggestion.
Another member suggested they give him thirty thousand
pounds.

The Opposition supported this figure and so did Sir Robert Peel. And when this amount was put to vote, it passed by
a majority of 262 votes to 158. This meant that Albert would
receive twenty thousand pounds less than the others who
had been in similar circumstances.

Victoria was furious.

Getting out her diary, she confided to its pages what she
thought about those who would not give her Albert a high
title and who were parsimonious with his income. She described Peel as a "low hypocrite." The Tories in general were
labeled "infernal scoundrels." The Bishop of Exeter was a
"fiend." Her New Year's prayer was grim: "From the Tories,
good Lord deliver us!" Since the Duke of Wellington was a
Tory she even lost some of her love for him.

The Duchess of Kent insisted that it would be indecent
for Albert to spend the night under the same roof as Victoria
on the day before their wedding. Victoria disagreed. After all,
the large palace had plenty of separate rooms for each of
them. Victoria was totally innocent, and so was Albert. In
thankfulness for her purity, she mailed fifty pounds to Eliz-

---

[1]*Letters of the Prince Consort*, p. 34.

abeth Fry at the Manor Hall Refuge of Destitute Females.

After dinner on February 9, Victoria sat between Albert and Lord Melbourne as they played a game which emphasized guessing words.

Before retiring, Victoria noted in her diary that this would be the last night she slept alone.

In contrast to the magnificent weather London had enjoyed during her coronation—weather which had been dubbed the Queen's Weather—rain drenched the city. In the morning, she sent a note to Albert. "What weather!" But, she added, "I believe . . . the rain will cease. Send one word when you, my most dearly beloved bridegroom, will be ready."

She wrote in her journal:

> Got up at ¼ to 9—well, and having slept well and break-fasted at ½ p. 9. Mamma came before and brought me a Nosegay of orange flowers. My dearest kindest Lehzen gave me a dear little ring. . . . Had my hair dressed and the wreath of orange flowers put on. . . . At ½ p. 12 I set off, dearest Albert having gone before. I wore a white satin gown with a very deep flounce of Honiton lace. . . . I wore my Turkish diamond necklace and earrings, and Albert's beautiful sapphire broach. Mamma and the Duchess of Sutherland went in the carriage with me. I never saw such crowds of people as there were in the Park, and they cheered enthusiastically. . . . The Flourish of Trumpets ceased as I entered the Chapel.[2]

The wedding could have been in the larger and far more impressive Westminster Abbey. But Victoria insisted on the much smaller Chapel Royal at St. James's. An unspoken reason for her decision was that Chapel Royal was not big enough to seat "those dreadful Tories." Melbourne had chided her for not inviting members of the Opposition; and, because of him, she had relented and mailed invitations to the Duke of Wellington and Lord Liverpool.

"Aren't you going to invite Sir Robert Peel?" asked Melbourne, suppressing a smile.

"Never!" replied Victoria.

Each of the Chapel seats had been trimmed in gold and

---

crimson. The entire cabinet, as well as five hundred peers and peeresses, together with many ambassadors and the entire Royal household filled every seat. All dressed in their very finest.

At 12:25 trumpets sounded, indicating the groom's procession approached. Splendid in his Field Marshall's uniform and with the star and ribbon of the Garter on his chest, Prince Albert caught every eye as he slowly advanced forward.

Ten minutes later, Melbourne with the Sword of State held vertically in his hands, led the bridal procession. Members of the Royal Family followed him. Then came Victoria. In addition to her Turkish diamond necklace, scattered diamonds sparkled in her hair. She wore the Collar of the Garter around her neck.

Each of the twelve bridesmaids, dressed in white, had difficulty holding on to the train of white satin and marching behind the Queen. They carried bouquets of roses.

At the altar, Victoria joined Albert who held a Bible bound in green velvet. Both of them knelt for a moment of quiet prayer. Then they took their places before the Archbishop of Canterbury. The task of giving the bride away fell to the Duke of Sussex who insisted on wearing a black skullcap. (When questioned, he insisted that it kept his head warm.)

Baroness Louise Lehzen wore a black velvet hat and white plume which attracted considerable attention. She sat in a position where she could see and hear every fragment of the ceremony. Lehzen silently prayed there would be no mishaps.

The Duke of Cambridge, Victoria's uncle, not only listened, but kept mumbling audible comments as well.

When the Archbishop asked the normal questions used in a marriage ceremony, each answered in modest tones. The Queen's voice had the identical musical timbre it had when she spoke in the House of Lords. When Albert was asked, "Do you take this woman to be your wife?", Victoria turned and looked him full in the face when he said, "I will."

The instant Albert placed the ring on Victoria's finger, a battery of guns fired a salute.

After they had been pronounced man and wife, Albert led

her by the hand to the Throne Room. There, the Royal Family and the Coburgs placed their signatures in the official Registry Book. Their signatures recorded, the relatives of both the bride and the groom proceeded on to Buckingham Palace where a wedding "breakfast" had been prepared.

The wedding cake was three feet in diameter, weighed three hundred pounds, and cost one hundred guineas (about five hundred dollars). A statue of Britannia stood in the center of the cake with a number of cupids positioned around her feet.

The bride and groom headed for Windsor Castle at 4 P.M. As the gilded carriage sped away, Charles Greville grumbled because it was not the best carriage. Victoria and Albert, however, didn't notice that it wasn't the best. They had each other! Even so, they managed to smile and wave at the crowds.

In a leading paragraph, the Times summed the occasion:

> On Monday, 10 February 1840, in the Chapel Royal at St. James's, Victoria of the United Kingdom of Great Britain and Ireland, Queen, Defender of the Faith, Sovereign of the Orders of the Garter, Thistle, Bath, St. Patrick, St. Michael and St. George, married to His Royal Highness Francis-Albert-Augustus, Charles-Emmanuel, Duke of Saxe, Prince of Coburg and Gotha, K.G.[3]

After the carriage had stopped at the gate of Windsor Castle, Albert assisted Victoria in her descent from the carriage. Then, arm in arm, they entered the historic building and inspected their apartment. It had been exquisitely furnished. But, as they went from room to room, Albert became disturbed. "Why is it," he asked, "that Lehzen's bedroom opens right off from your dressing room?"

"I guess that's the way the architect planned it."

"But why?"

"Baroness Lehzen became my governess when I was five. She's been with me since that time. That means fifteen years! We're very close."

"Do you still need her?" Albert frowned.

---

[3] *Victoria and Albert*, 1977, p. 157.

"W-well, n-no. But . . ."

"Then why should she stay?" He peered into her face and smiled.

Ignoring his question, Victoria said, "I think I'd better go into the bedroom and change into something more comfortable."

Having donned a plain dress, Victoria returned to the living room. There, she found Albert sitting at the piano wearing his Windsor coat.

"You're a fine pianist," she murmured as she sat on the seat beside him.

"I do love music, especially Bach. But Luther's compositions are among my favorites. Listen!" He played *A Mighty Fortress is My God*. "That's my favorite. When I was a boy, I visited the Wartburg Castle. That's where Luther hid from his enemies and translated the New Testament into German."

"Did you see the splotch of ink on the wall where Luther threw his inkwell at the devil?"

"Of course, but that was nearly three hundred years ago and the ink is rather faded."

"Do you think it's ever renewed?" She laughed.

"Of course. But my love for you never has to be renewed." He took her into his arms. Then he held her on his lap until dinner was announced.

After they had bowed their heads and thanked the Lord for the food, Victoria smiled at him across the table. "You know, Albert dear, this is the first time we've eaten alone since we were married. It's a historic occasion."

"That it is."

Victoria had taken only a few bites when she began to feel desperately ill. "I-I'm afraid I can't eat anything," she managed as she got up and laid on the sofa. "My head is about to burst."

"It has been a busy day," sympathized Albert, sitting by her side.

But ill or not, Victoria was happy. A glance at her diary for the 11th indicates how she felt.

. . . ill or not, I NEVER NEVER spent such an evening!!! My DEAREST DEAREST DEAR Albert sat on a footstool by my side, & his excessive love & affection gave me feelings of heavenly love & happiness, I never could have hoped to have felt before!—really how can I ever be thankful enough to have such a Husband![4]

The next morning they got up "at ¼ to 8." After breakfast "I walked with my precious Angel, all alone—so delightful, on the Terrace and new Walk, arm in arm. . . . We talked a great deal together. We came home at one and had luncheon soon after. Poor dear Albert felt sick and uncomfortable and lay down in my room. . . . He looked so dear, lying there and dozing . . ."[5]

Albert was soon feeling better. The next day, still quivering in ecstasy, Victoria confided to her diary, "Already the 2nd day since our marriage; his love and gentleness is beyond everything, and to kiss that dear soft cheek, to press my lips to his, is heavenly bliss. I feel a purer more unearthly feel than I ever did. Oh! was ever woman so blessed as I am."[6]

Even though Queen Victoria did not *rule*, it took considerable effort to *reign*. Each day required that she read reports, listen to ambassadors, consult with Melbourne and sign documents—hundreds and hundreds of documents.

Albert, on the other hand, had no official tasks. True, he had to be seen with the Queen, lay a few cornerstones, appear at luncheons and wave at the crowds when he and the Queen were in public together. But no one ever consulted him on any important matter at any time. Victoria sensed his unhappiness and she had a solution. Faced with a stack of documents to sign, she said, "Albert dear, I need your help."

"Yes, Your Majesty," he teased. "I'm at your service."

The Queen waved at a high stack of documents. "I have to sign each one and it would be most helpful if you would blot my signature."

[4]*Queen Victoria, Born to Succeed*, 1964, p. 143.
[5]Ibid., p. 64.
[6]Ibid., p. 65.

Albert smiled. "Let's get started so we won't delay the opera," he said, picking up the blotter.

After he had blotted about twenty Victoria R. signatures, he had a question. "Your Majesty, have you read all these documents?"

"Not word for word. But I've glanced at all of them. I don't want to make the mistake Queen Elizabeth claimed she made."

"What was that?"

"She claimed that without realizing what she did, she signed Mary Queen of Scots' death warrant."

"Do you believe that?" A doubtful smile crinkled his lips.

"It is hard to believe. Nonetheless, I don't want to make a similar mistake." She picked up another document.

After he had applied the blotter a dozen more times, Albert had another question. "Your Majesty, am I allowed to attend cabinet meetings?"

"I'm afraid not."

"Why?"

"Because I'm the Queen and you—you are merely my husband."

Albert froze, the blotter in midair. "What, then, am I supposed to do?" he demanded angrily.

"You are supposed to love me and—and—and—"

"And father your children," he concluded.

"Yes, that's right. And I'm afraid you've already been successful."

"We've only been married three months! Are you with child?"

"I'm afraid so. I guess I was caught."

"What do you mean, you're *afraid so*? Don't you want to be a mother?"

"I do. But I'd hoped we could live together for a year before that happened." She sighed.

"And what do you want it to be?"

"A princess."

"I don't. I want it to be the Prince of Wales!" He bent over and kissed her. "When's it due?"

"Doctor Clark said it would be sometime in December."

"Mmmm. Are you feeling all right?"

"Of course. But I'll feel better when I get all of these horrid documents signed and we're on our way to the opera."

He picked her up and held her on his lap.

12
Despair

Albert's unhappiness increased. Blotting Victoria's signature was not enough to give him a sense of value. Another problem added to his feeling of helplessness. As the Queen's pregnancy advanced, she occasionally succumbed to morning sickness. On these occasions, Lehzen was generally first at her bed.

Being a realist, Albert decided he must solve some of his problems on his own.

While rummaging in the library at Windsor, he accidentally picked up a discarded folio of drawings by Hans Holbein and Leonardo da Vinci. Leafing through it, he realized they were priceless. Later, he discovered bundles of letters that had been written by, and to, kings and queens. These items became a challenge.

Methodically, he filed and indexed them so they would not be lost. This work gave him a glowing sense of accomplishment.

That project completed, he began to improve the stables. He kept men busy until the stables were among the finest in Europe. Glowing with pride, he showed Victoria around the renovated buildings and explained what he had been doing. "And now that we've improved the stables," he told her, "we must improve our horses."

"And how do we do that?" She gripped his arm.

"By breeding. If we want a first class racehorse we must breed a first class racehorse mare to a first class racehorse stallion. If we want the best draft horses to work the farms, we must breed in a likewise manner."

"Sounds interesting."

Albert pointed at Pegasus, a magnificent stallion who had just been presented to the Queen. "He's really a great horse, perhaps the best in Europe. I'm going to breed him to our finest racehorse mares. Soon, we'll have some colts that can almost fly."

On their way back to the castle, Victoria looked up at him and asked, "Do the same breeding principles work with human beings?"

"Of course. A stunted man married to a stunted woman will probably have stunted children. And a brilliant man married to a brilliant woman will probably have brilliant children."

Victoria rushed toward a bench. "I must sit down," she groaned. She closed her eyes and gritted her teeth. "I must have a touch of morning sickness. Oooh!"

After a few minutes, she took Albert's hand into both of hers. Then, while studying his face, she said, "I have another question. If a man is insane, is there a chance that some of his children will be insane?"

"Of course. Insanity, like harelips, is often relayed from one generation to another."

"Like the color of the hair, or shape of the nose?"

"That's right."

Victoria looked worried. "Could insanity skip a generation?"

"What do you mean?"

"If a grandfather were insane, could his great-grandchildren also be insane?"

Albert gazed into the distance, thinking. "I suppose so. But I'm not a doctor. Why do you ask?"

"Oh, never mind." She became intensely quiet for a long time. Then she slowly got to her feet. "I-I'm not f-f-feeling well," she stammered. "I'm afraid you'd better help me get back to the apartment."

Albert looked worried. "Is it something you ate?"

"I-I d-don't know."

"Can you walk?"

"If you help me."

Slowly, and after resting on three benches along the way, they managed to get to the castle. There, they rested for a long time before making their way to their apartment. While sinking into an overstuffed chair, Victoria remarked, "I feel so tired, so terribly tired."

"Just relax," replied Albert. "Carrying babies isn't the easiest thing."

"You mean I'm going to have twins?"

Both of them laughed.

While she relaxed, a servant placed a tray of letters on a nearby stand. Fumbling through them, Victoria found one from the Post Office. Excitedly, she exclaimed, "Albert, look at this!"

She held up a square wrapper with a triangular flap and shook it. "I've no idea what it is. I'll read the instructions."

The enclosed statement indicated this new piece of merchandise was an "envelope." She had never heard this word before. *No longer do we need to fold our letters and then seal them with a dab of wax*, read the instructions. *Now all we need to do is to put the letter in an envelope, moisten the triangular flap and press it down. The flap can be moistened with either water or saliva. When pressed down, it will stick to the other part of the envelope. The address should then be written on the front.*

Albert laughed, then produced a newly invented one-penny stamp. It featured the Queen's profile. He licked it and placed it on the envelope. "Our world is surely changing," he commented. "Now we have stamps, envelopes, steam engines and gaslights. I've been told that Michael Faraday has changed magnetism into electricity." He shook his head. "Maybe someday we'll even have electric lights."

Victoria only half listened to Albert. An interesting letter captured most of her attention. "This concerns you," she announced. "Listen! You have been requested to make a speech against slavery."

"I thought we had abolished slavery," replied Albert, reaching for the letter.

"We abolished the Trade in 1807 and we freed the slaves in our own colonies in 1833. But the Arabs refuse to give it up. Right now, while I speak, the slave market in Zanzibar is overflowing with men, women and children who are being sold at auction."

"Do you think I should accept their invitation?"

"Of course. Britain has the largest navy in the world. We should use it to stop the slave trade. That is one of our God-assigned duties."

Albert strode away, slapping the letter against his palm. "But I don't know much about slavery. And my German is much better than my English."

Victoria walked up to him, putting her hand on his arm. "Never mind. The library is filled with books on slavery. I just saw a new biography of William Wilberforce. I'll help you with your English."

Albert hesitated.

"You will be speaking to at least five thousand people. You can help change history."

"If you vill help, I vill do it," teased Albert, deliberately using the dialect of a German trying to speak English. "Da power of a voman is wery great. Especially dat of my vife, Queen Wictoria."

Albert carefully selected books on slavery, read the biography of Wilberforce, visited his grave in Westminster Abbey, and read some of his speeches. Each day his interests flamed higher and higher. Finally, he sat down and wrote the speech. Then he faced Victoria. "Now I will read it to you," he said, holding the manuscript to the light.

Victoria listened as he read his speech. "The content is very good," she complimented. "But I think it could be far more effective if you were to give it without the use of your manuscript."

"You mean I should memorize it?" Albert's jaw sagged.

"At least you should memorize the main outline."

Albert followed her advice. Soon even the squirrels at Windsor paused with acorns in their paws as Albert informed them about the horrors of slavery and how the British Navy should be used to help suppress the traffic.

When Albert faced the crowded hall jammed with anti-slavers on June 1, he was terrified. But as he spoke and visualized slave auctions in Zanzibar, his mind cleared. Soon he had departed from parts of his speech and captivated the crowd's attention. When he concluded, the entire audience leaped to its feet and made every window in the place vibrate with prolonged cheers.

The response lifted Albert's spirits. *Perhaps there were more things for him to do than to be nice to Victoria, father princes and princesses, and lay cornerstones!*

Several days after this triumph, Victoria and Albert headed out of Buckingham Palace on their way to visit her mother. While going up Constitution Hill, two pistol shots shattered the quiet evening. From a spot only a few yards away, on the Green Park side of the street, an eighteen-year-old bartender from Birmingham had taken deliberate aim and fired. The shots from both pistols lodged themselves in the garden wall.

A hysterical crowd immediately surrounded the assailant, screaming, "Kill him! Kill him!" Had it not been for the police, he would have been torn apart.

Albert, sitting between Victoria and the would-be assassin, witnessed the entire episode. Victoria accepted the matter calmly. She even laughed. The crowd responded by surrounding her carriage and escorting her back to the palace.

The bartender, Edward Oxford, was found insane by the courts.

During his next conference with the Queen, Melbourne approached her with a serious proposition. He explained that a bill should be presented to Parliament which would decree that in case of her death, Albert would immediately become the Regent. Without such a bill, the next in line would be the Duke of Cumberland. This man with his hideous face and grasping personality lived as the most despised male offspring of George III.

Victoria understood.

They immediately worked out the bill and submitted it to Parliament. It passed with a minimum of debate. Albert was immensely pleased.

By studying some musty volumes, Melbourne learned that Queen Anne's husband had been allowed to accompany her when she addressed Parliament, that he attended important meetings and that he had been allowed to read the dispatches. Since these privileges had been extended to Queen Anne's husband, Melbourne insisted they be extended to Albert.

"You are winning your way," congratulated Victoria as she stood by a cold fireplace.

Albert smiled.

"But I do wish you could get the right people to light the fireplaces early in the morning so we could be warm. Brrr!"

"I thought the British liked cold houses . . ."

"We do. But not this cold. If the assassins don't get me, pneumonia will."

Albert's investigations proved an amazingly inefficient bureaucracy tied up both Buckingham Palace and Windsor Castle. The responsibility for firewood rested on one set of bureaucrats, while the responsibility for lighting the firewood belonged to another set of bureaucrats. Even worse, neither set cooperated with the other. This organized confusion typified other systematic confusion.

Candles represented another major problem. All the rooms, Albert learned, were supplied with candles. Each day the supply of candles was renewed, even though the previous day's supply had not been exhausted. The unused candles, together with the partially burned ones, were sold and the money disappeared into a bureaucrat's pocket.

Other problems included matches and toilet tissue. Most

of the rooms had an adequate supply of candles. Few had matches. Each lavatory was supplied with conveniently cut squares snipped from the *Times*, the *Morning Chronicle*, or one of the other newspapers.

Albert was horrified. It was a disgrace that the palaces of the world's best-known Queen should be supplied with such items.

Albert kept explaining these problems to both Melbourne and Victoria. Even while he expounded on them, Victoria complained about the cold. "We *must* have fire in these fire-places," she wailed. "Those bureaucrats *must* get together. If they don't, I'll freeze to death or have a miscarriage."

Sometimes she wept.

After a lot of bitterly cold nights and teeth-chattering days, Victoria sat alone in the living room. Dressed in an overcoat, with Dash on her lap, she squeezed as close to the fireless fireplace as possible. While shivering, wave after wave of pessimism swept over her. Each of her troubles danced before her like animated skeletons in a museum. Unable to keep them out of her mind, she pondered over each of them.

One major problem involved her mother. The Duchess existed in unhappiness because she had to live in a separate building, and thus could not barge in on Victoria whenever she had the impulse.

A more serious worry centered on Melbourne. He had been like a father to her. He had coached her, written her speeches, encouraged her. But now his government tottered. It was evident he would be forced to resign. His resignation would mean the Tories—the horrible Tories—would be in power. And even worse, the dreadful Tories would be headed by no other than Sir Robert Peel. Ugh!

Lehzen represented another concern. Victoria loved her and wanted her to remain. But Albert was determined she should retire. Victoria realized he had good reasons to feel that way. Having made major decisions in the royal residences for years, Lehzen could not force herself to accept the fact that many of these decisions should be made by Albert. Caught in a dilemma, Victoria knew she would suffer regardless of what happened.

While pondering these and other troubles, Albert stepped in. Three workmen accompanied him, their arms loaded with firewood. "I've decided to go over the heads of the bureaucrats," he announced. "From now on, we're going to have a warm apartment whether they like it or not."

"Amen!" responded Victoria, moving back from the dead fireplace.

After the apartment had become toasty, Albert said, "I've found something I know you'll enjoy. It had been tucked away in some memos which concerned your grandfather, George III." He spread a cartoon on a table. "This was published in April, 1819."

The cartoon depicted the Dukes of Clarence, Cambridge, Kent and Cumberland. Each stood behind or by the side of his pregnant wife. After carefully studying the drawing, Victoria commented, "The pressure on the dukes to produce a legitimate heir was enormous. An heir was desperately needed to continue the Hanoverian line. They were the only ones capable of producing such an heir." She picked up the page and held it to the light.

She studied the cartoonist's version of her mother and father. "Look, I'm the one who made my mother's abdomen so enormous," she said.

Victoria handed the cartoon back to Albert. She sat, intensely quiet, for a long time.

"What's the matter?" asked Albert.

"I was wondering what our role in life actually is. I'm the Queen, but I have no power. You are my husband and you have no power. Could it be that we are good for nothing but to breed children?"

"Don't be so pessimistic," replied Albert. "You have a lot of power. Sir Robert Peel had to resign as Prime Minister because of you."

"True. But a few days later, the people booed me."

He threw his up head and looked startled. "Why?"

"Because as Queen, I'm supposed to be neutral! I have to read speeches whether I like them or not. I have to sign documents whether I agree with their contents or not. I even had to invite Tories to our wedding!"

She stood up and walked around the room. "Albert, I have another question. It's a question that has been worrying me a lot in the last day or two." She fixed her eyes on him. "Now, I want you to tell me the truth. Please don't hedge." She returned to her seat near the fireplace. "A few weeks ago, we talked about the breeding of horses. You explained that a stallion's son is generally much like him. I understand that. But what about the dominant characteristics of a distant relative—say, ten or fifteen generations before? Could they show up in the latest offspring?"

"I'm not an expert. But I know sometimes they do."

"Mmmm. Could some of the characteristics of my relatives many generations back show up in our child?"

"I imagine they could."

"That worries me."

Albert leaned toward her and touched her hand. "Why?"

"Some of my relatives were—let's be kind—some of them were rather colorful people."

"For example?"

Victoria sat up straight in the chair. "Mary Tudor, the eldest daughter of Henry VIII. She was so wicked, we call her Bloody Queen Mary. On Maundy Thursday, she washed the feet of some of London's poorest beggars. Then, a few days later, she condemned a handful of Anabaptists to be burned at the stake. Mary ordered Protestants burned with as little thought as we order tea. She. . . ."

Victoria suddenly stopped and clutched at her abdomen. "It's kicking! The baby's kicking!" she cried. Her eyes brightened with wonder.

After the baby had quieted, Albert said, "Mary Tudor would have been overjoyed if her baby had kicked."

"What do you mean?"

"I read about her when I was a boy. Realizing that she could not accomplish all her goals in her lifetime, Mary desperately wanted an heir. And, for a time, she convinced herself she would become a mother.

"Even though her abdomen continued getting bigger and

bigger, she did not have a baby. She wasn't even pregnant. Why? Because God had decided to spare us from other rulers who would be like her. From the writings of Luther and my own observation, I'm convinced that God still rules."

"I believe that. Nonetheless, the wickedness that flowed through her bloodstream may still be in mine. It may be infecting this baby right now."

"How could that be?" A tone of sarcasm spread through his voice. "You're not even one of Mary's descendants!"

"But her father's bloodline flowed through all the Stuarts into the Hanoverians. That includes me. Think about my distant ancestor Charles II, also a Stuart. His court was an open sewer—the most corrupt court England has ever seen. In addition to his own immorality, he did some hideous things."

She clutched at her abdomen and then hesitated. "It's kicking again." She smiled. "It's quit now. Don't worry. I'm all right."

Albert looked carefully at his wife. "What were some of the hideous things he did?"

"Did you ever hear what he did to the corpse of Oliver Cromwell?"

"Tell me."

"He had it extracted from Westminster Abbey, dragged through the city to Tyburn on a sled, then hung on a gallows. After the masses saw it, he ordered the head chopped off. They placed the head on a pole where it was displayed for twenty years from the top of Westminster Hall."

Albert's face twisted in disgust. "How horrible!"

"Yes, it is horrible. But even more horrible is the fact that I'm related to him. And this baby that's kicking inside of me is also related to him." Her face turned sour and she visibly shuddered.

"Are you feeling all right?" asked Albert, putting his arms around her shoulders.

"I'm feeling fine. But I want you to have a look at a couple other skeletons in our royal closet. Queen Anne was the daughter of James II, who was the brother of Charles II. Anne was not immoral or corrupt, nor did she send anyone to the stake. But she loathed Catholics, Baptists, Quakers, Presbyterians, Independents, and all other Dissenters as much as Mary Tudor hated Protestants. The only church she believed in was the Church of England.

"Queen Anne, this relative of mine! had the Schism Act passed. It forbade any Dissenter from teaching public school."

"And what happened to her Schism Act?" A mischievous smile crinkled the corners of Albert's lips.

"She died the very day it was supposed to go into effect."

"And what happened to her children, her potential heirs?"

"They died, all seventeen of them."

"And who came into power?"

"The Hanoverians."

"And what did the first of them, George I, do to the Schism Act?"

"He abolished it."

Albert's smile widened. "And so God had his way. Right?"

"But the Georges were not all saints," snapped Victoria. "George I and George II were as immoral as it is possible to be. Grandfather, George III, claimed he lost his mind because William Pitt wanted to allow Catholics to serve in the army as officers.

"My uncles, George IV and William IV were strange men. So was my father and most of his brothers. Remember how Uncle Augustus wore a black skullcap at our wedding even though he gave me away?" she laughed.

"Oh, but he needed it to keep his head warm!" replied Albert a little sarcastically.

"They're all spendthrifts and woman chasers. Had not Parliament paid their debts, they'd be bankrupt. My own father wasted money as if it were valueless. And he was cruel. When he was in charge of the army at Malta, he sentenced a man to be flogged with nine hundred and ninety-nine lashes. Then he watched as the sentence was carried out!"

Victoria sucked in her breath. "Even so, he was my father. Had it not been for him, I would not be Queen."

Albert stood up. "Well, Your Majesty, you've rattled a lot of skeletons. But keep in mind that there are a few piles of bones in my own closet. My father—God bless him!—is still a spendthrift, a woman chaser and a drunk. That's one reason King Leopold and I only drink water! And my mother left my father for an army officer.

"Nonetheless, Your Majesty, the good Lord has given each of us a special position in which we can do an immense amount of good. Both of us have been born of the Spirit and that means everything. Moreover, we are joint-heirs with Christ. Think of it. *Joint-heirs*!"

He pointed at their canary who outdid himself singing in his golden cage. "Just listen to him. He's caged, yet he sings. Why? Because he's fulfilling his God-given duty. We can do the same."

He kissed her and put on his hat. "I must rush over to the stables," he explained as he stepped out the door.

At about 2 A.M. on November 21, a sharp pain awakened Victoria. When another followed a few minutes later, she alerted Albert. "I think my time has come," she said. "Summon the doctors and have the Archbishop of Canterbury notified."

As the doctors hurried up the stairs to her apartment, Victoria's condition concerned them, for the baby had decided to arrive three weeks early.

13

Opium and Pigtails

Between pains, Victoria thought about Queen Adelaide. One of her babies had also come early. Born at Calais while Adelaide and William were on their way to London, the baby did not survive.

Ten hours passed in endless dragging minutes. The pains grew stronger with each hour, tightening, pressing inward. She turned her mind to Princess Charlotte.

Queen-to-be Charlotte had continued in labor for forty-eight hours only to have the baby stillborn. Had her baby lived, he would have been the Prince of Wales and the present king. And Charlotte. The two-day struggle had been too much for her. She passed away within a few hours. *Did a similar fate await her?*

"Oh God," she prayed, "help me."

From the nearby room, Victoria could hear the soft murmur of voices, and among them she recognized the deep tones of the Archbishop. Albert stood nearby. What would she ever do without Albert? Whenever she needed him, he was present. In the middle of a pain, she squeezed his hand.

Again and again, she heard Doctor Locock say, "You're doing fine. You're doing fine. Everything is all right."

As the pain increased to a wrenching intensity, she felt herself lean forward, drawn by an unseen force. "Now, Your Majesty," Doctor Locock encouraged, "you must push. That's right. Push, push, push. A little more. A little more. That's fine, you can do it."

With a strong push and a surge of relief, Victoria ended her twelve-hour labor at 1:40 P.M. She looked up at Doctor Locock. "It's a fine healthy princess," he announced.

Minutes later, the Queen provided the new heir to the British Crown her first afternoon lunch. The baby must have enjoyed it, for she drifted into sleep almost immediately. As she did, the church bells all over London boomed the good news.

The fact that both the Queen and the princess had survived, thus placing two barriers between the Duke of Cumberland and the Throne, caused everyone to rejoice. Soon hacks scribbled pieces of doggerel. One of the best concerned the doctors:

> Doctors Locock, Bladgen, Clark, They made the great discovery, And having brought the goods to town, Were paid upon delivery.

Victoria recovered quickly. Albert remained near to her during her convalescence. He read to her, supplied her every want and made certain she was warm.

Before the christening of the Royal Princess, Victoria referred to her as "the Child."

At first, the Royal Princess seemed a little thin. She soon gained so much weight the doctors no longer worried. When the Queen recovered, she had Albert's desk placed beside hers. From then on, he knew that he was a part, a very minor part, of the reigning team.

Because Her Majesty did not have the time to be constantly nursing the little princess, she employed a wet nurse. This lady, the wife of a professional man, quite appropriately came from the nearby port of Cowes. She received one thousand pounds for her services and the little princess fell in love with her. Within the first six weeks, the busy Queen only got to see her baby bathed twice.

Early one December morning, a squeak of a door startled the Queen's nurse. Thoroughly alarmed, she slipped the bolt in place and shouted for one of the Queen's pages.

The page searched the living room for an intruder. Without finding one, he looked under the couch. Shrugging his shoulders, he said, "Whoever it was, 'e must 'ave disappeared."

Lehzen, however, who had also joined in the search, did not give up. She pushed the couch aside. There, curled in a ball, crouched a dirty-faced eighteen-year-old boy. Eyes wide, she almost screamed.

The page seized the culprit immediately and summoned the police. While in custody, the lad, known as "the Boy Jones," confessed that he had done a similar thing in 1838. He had climbed a wall, crept through a window, sat upon the throne, saw the Queen and heard the Princess Royal cry. Because they felt he was insane, the authorities were merciful to him, allowing him to escape prison by going to sea.

Thoroughly alarmed, for she had been sitting on that same couch a mere three hours before, Queen Victoria decided the palace had to be thoroughly renovated—and soon. Albert wanted to start making changes immediately. Lehzen, the heroine of the day, had ideas about the proposed renovation that didn't agree with his. Annoyed, Albert made up his mind that as soon as Lehzen's triumph was forgotten, he would press for her dismissal.

The year 1840 ended with a deep sorrow for Victoria. Her little dog Dash unexpectedly passed away. Months later, a marble likeness was placed over his grave at Adelaide Cottage. His epitaph reads:

Here lies
DASH
The favourite spaniel of Her Majesty Queen Victoria
In his 10th Year
His attachment was without selfishness
His playfulness without malice
His fidelity without deceit
READER
If you would be beloved and die regretted
Profit by the example of
DASH

Victoria arranged for her daughter's christening to be on February 10—the first anniversary of their wedding.

Albert's father, Duke Ernest, did not bother to reply to the letter which invited him to be his granddaughter's godfather. (The supposition is that he was piqued because Victoria had not arranged for him to have a pension.) When it became apparent that her father-in-law did not plan to come, Victoria invited the Duke of Wellington to take his place.

Planning together, the Queen and Albert decided their princess would enter in the arms of former Queen Adelaide. And, for this solemn occasion, Albert composed an inspiring chorale. Just as Adelaide began her slow march forward to the font, an inadvertently opened door revealed the splendidly uniformed Duke of Wellington. Seeing him, the orchestra immediately dropped Albert's chorale and struck up with "See the Conquering Hero Comes." This lively march was followed by three cheers.

Suppressing a smile, Adelaide handed the princess to Victoria. The Archbishop of Canterbury baptized her as Victoria Adelaide Mary Louise. The newly christened princess seemed to enjoy the entire ceremony. She even cooed at the conclusion.

In the months following the christening, Victoria secretly ground her teeth in her efforts to remain neutral politically. She watched as the Whigs were slowly whittled down by the Tories under the relentless pressure of Robert Peel.

Since Melbourne, as stubborn as ever, refused to resign, Victoria had the distasteful task of dissolving Parliament on June 23. Secretly, she hoped the election would give the Whigs a majority. Her hopes were shattered. The Tories swept the country. Melbourne was out and Peel was in.

Victoria was heartsick.

On August 24, the Queen expressed her grief in a letter to King Leopold:

> You don't say that you sympathize with me in my present heavy trial, the heaviest I have ever had to endure, and which will be a sad heart-breaking to me—but I know you do feel

for me. I am quite prepared, but still I feel very sad, and God knows! very wretched at times, for myself and my country, that such a change must take place. But God in His mercy will support and guide me through all. Yet I feel that my constant headaches are caused by annoyance and vexation![1]

In his later years, Melbourne had fallen into the habit of dozing—and sometimes snoring!—at banquets. Nonetheless, Queen Victoria invited him to the palace for a farewell dinner in honor of his services. While reminiscing on the terrace beneath a sky bright with stars, he murmured, "It is painful for me. During the last four years I have seen you daily and I like it better every day."

She offered him the Garter. He refused on the grounds that he never accepted honors. Instead, she gave him some personal etchings which he appreciated.

Home was no less tumultuous. Louise Lehzen seemed to always be at the center of the conflict. Few who knew Louise Lehzen were neutral about her. In the Royal residences, the people either loved or hated her.

Victoria kept her on a pinnacle and referred to her as "My dearly beloved angelic Lehzen."[2] But Albert never became reconciled to her. To him, she was "The House dragon spitting fire." He even insisted that she was "a crazy, common, stupid intriguer."

The conflict came to a climax when Vicky—the shortened name for the new princess—began to cut teeth.

On their return from Claremont, Victoria and Albert discovered that Vicky was not well. Albert blamed Lehzen. "You've been feeding her an improper diet," he accused.

"You're wrong," replied Lehzen heatedly. "I've been giving her exactly what the doctor prescribed."

Infuriated, Albert increased his campaign to get rid of Lehzen.

One accusation inspired another accusation. Soon the

---

[1] *Queen Victoria in Her Letters and Journals*, 1985, pp. 67–68.
[2] Ibid., p. 35.

Prince and the Queen were glaring, then shouting at each other.

As the storm lashed, Victoria discovered she was pregnant again. Consulting the calendar, she was horrified to note that her first two babies would be a mere eleven and half months apart. She was furious.

She did not have time to linger over these frustrations, for she now faced another: that of getting along with the new Prime Minister, Sir Robert Peel.

Coached by Melbourne, Victoria quickly learned Peel was not the ogre she had imagined. Indeed, he had certain charms even though he was an out and out Tory.

During a calm that settled over her apprehension of Peel and the war between Albert and Lehzen, Victoria's steps began to firm. Her morning sickness slacked off and she began to feel faint but strong movements within. Since she had successfully delivered Vicky, she felt confident that her second delivery would be much easier. Besides, problems of the country were more pressing than her second pregnancy.

For many years Britain had a trade imbalance with China. Britain had paid China nearly thirty million pounds in silver and gold for tea, but had only been able to sell them a little over nine million pounds worth of British products.

In an effort to remedy this, the British searched for a product which they could sell to the Chinese. Each product they presented to them was rejected. After all, an Englishman who had spent much of his life in China explained, "The Chinese have the best food in the world, rice, the best drink, tea, the best clothing, cotton, silk and furs. They do not need to buy a penny's worth elsewhere."[3]

The British were dismayed, but they refused to give up. Soon they learned they had control of an item which could so addict a person, the victim would sell his soul in order to get another pinch.

That item was opium.

---

[3] *The Chinese Opium Wars*, 1975, p. 17.

For many years, the Chinese had imported small amounts of opium for medicinal purposes. Opium smoking, on the other hand, was illegal. The British, however, found ingenious ways to keep supplying the drug to the Chinese.

In spite of drastic laws and severe penalties, the importation of opium continued to escalate. And each year thousands of wretches shortened their lives by lingering in the opium dens. An investigation in 1813 revealed that even some of the Imperial Guard and court eunuchs had become addicted.

Hoping to terrify importers, an object lesson was arranged. It was bannered that Ho Lao-chin, keeper of an opium den, was to be publicly executed at 11 A.M. on December 12. The cross on which he was to die was dropped into a hole beneath the American flag which snapped in the breeze atop its one hundred foot staff.

As scores of foreigners craned their necks, Ho Lao-chin was dragged out of his cell by a heavy chain attached to an iron band around his neck. The executioners were in the act of locking his arms to othe cross when some Jack Tars showed up. Eager for excitement, they smashed the cross. Soon a mob of about eight thousand Chinese began heaving stones. Just before the riot turned into a massacre, two Americans managed to alert the police.

Even though no one was killed, a tiny flame had been kindled which was soon fanned into the first Opium War. The British continued to seek new ways to keep and increase their opium markets. The Chinese sought ways to bring the opium trade to a stop.

As tensions mounted, the Emperor appointed Lin Tse-hsu to investigate the ports where the opium was entering the country—and to do something about it. Lin, an educated man, moved to Canton and went to work. After issuing several strong edicts, he prepared a letter which was sent to Queen Victoria.

Lin's letter assumed that opium was illegal in England. He therefore suggested that she go over the heads of her administration and put a stop to its sale in China. His letter never reached her.

The frustrations of the Chinese and the flagrant defiance of the British escalated. Finally, the first shot was fired. Backed by a navy loaded with trained men, the British had the upper hand. Soon Chinhai and Ningpo were subdued and occupied. To many of the British, the entire operation was a lark. Some of them delighted in snipping off Chinese pigtails and mailing them to their girlfriends.

Since opium was legal in England, the masses could not understand why it should be banned in China. Moreover, the majority in Parliament viewed the trade with tolerance. After all, it was a lucrative business and produced a lot of money. And at the time, England needed money, lots and lots of money.

Queen Victoria was horrified at what was taking place. To her, it was neither fair, nor British.

14
Discovery

Victoria's troubles in the fall of 1841 continued to multiply. As October leaves in Green Park crimsoned, little Vicky's indigestion and loss of weight continued. Concerned about her survival, the doctors kept her on a sole diet of "asses milk." In addition to her digestive problems, she had an unusually hard time cutting teeth.

Along with worries about Vicky, Victoria feared having a miscarriage. There were several false alarms. In between these alarms, she was heartsick about the troubles in China. Since the war was so far away, many barely knew it existed. Others considered the conflict an amusing diversion and laughed about the pigtails they received in the mail. Many, however, were thoroughly disgusted. They believed England's honor was at stake.

Sir Robert Peel introduced a motion of censure in Parliament. Even though strong voices, including that of William Gladstone whose sister had been ruined by the drug, were for the motion, it lost by nine votes.

The Opium War remained a heavy weight, but Victoria had many other burdens. A major one continued to be Lehzen. She had prayed her former governess and Albert would become compatible. It seemed a useless effort. Neither communicated to the other. They reminded Victoria of a pair of tomcats.

Another burden was that of her mother. The Duchess seemed to have an insatiable appetite for titles. Victoria, in a position to confer titles, did not feel her mother deserved them. Still, she wanted her mother to be happy. Utterly frustrated about the matter, she didn't know what to do. Again and again she searched her mind for a solution. But a realistic solution never presented itself.

Just after breakfast on October 26, Victoria felt the time had come for her to give birth. Doctor Locock agreed. But it was merely a false alarm.

Seized by a combination of anxiety and despair, she found herself plunging into self-pity. All her troubles seemed to march in front of her. Hands in their pockets, their faces smug, each trouble stuck out its tongue and pointed an accusing finger.

As she stared into space with lackluster eyes, she saw her grandfather, George III, sitting in his chair. Dressed in his violet gown, his long white beard halfway down his chest, his eyes wild with fright. As she watched, the doctors placed leeches on his head and stomach. Then she listened as her uncles mocked him.

"You're an absolute nobody," assured her uncle William.

"You're worse than a nobody," added Uncle George. "It was because of you that we lost the American Colonies!"

As Victoria watched and listened in memory, she wondered when the insanity, which had twisted her grandfather, her uncles, her father and her father-in-law, would reach out its bony fingers and twist her, or even worse, one of her children.

She got up and stood before the window. The gardeners were raking leaves outside. *Yes, they were happier than she!* Viewing the piles of leaves they formed, she was almost jealous of them. Not a single one was a mere figurehead.

Shuffling back to her chair, she reflected that her happiest moments were when she was being creative. Indeed, she had received more joy when she sketched Dash than she ever received when publicly praised. Her sketches were more precious to her than her diamonds. The diamonds had been given to her. But she alone had created the sketches.

Again, she considered the considerable boredom of endless protocol. Watching subjects back out of a room after an audience and listening to them as they answered, *Yes Your Majesty, No Your Majesty,* was a form of hell even Dante had failed to describe.

Her argument with Sir Robert Peel regarding dismissing her Whig Ladies remained fresh in her mind. She remembered how, in his letter to her, he had used the words, "Your Majesty," thirty-four times!

Almost gagging on those words, she all but wished they had never been invented. Ah, but because she was willing to endure them and be a figurehead, she was well paid.

Victoria began to think about the disgraceful Opium War. She wished she could stop it. It was terrible to be so helpless. As her self-pity continued, she sank deeper and deeper into the slime of despair. Then a Mother Goose rhyme Lehzen had taught her flashed into her mind. Softly, she quoted to herself:

> *"Pussy-cat, Pussy-cat, where have you been?"*
> *"I've been to London to visit the Queen."*
> *"Pussy-cat, Pussy-cat, what did you there?"*
> *"I frightened a little mouse under her chair."*

Thoughtfully, she considered the career of that now famous cat. Many had ridiculed it, but it had accomplished at least one thing. It had frightened a mouse! Still, that was more than she had done, *and perhaps more than she would ever be able to do.*

Completely frustrated, she went to bed and picked up the book she had been reading on the One Hundred Years' War. That war which had lasted more than a century, she had learned, had been started by England's Edward III. Edward was convinced that he was the rightful king of France because his mother was a sister to three French kings who had died without male heirs. Landing in Holland, he had invaded France. There, his first battle was fought at Crécy in 1346.

The British were grossly outnumbered, but because of their use of the longbow which could shoot four times faster than the French crossbow, they won a crushing victory. Their victory led to the fall of Calais.

Fascinated, Victoria skipped a few chapters until she came to the one which described the Battle of Agincourt fought in 1415. There, again, thanks to the longbow, a mere thirteen thousand Englishmen defeated fifty thousand Frenchmen. She was thinking about this when Albert returned.

"And what has your Majesty been doing?" he asked, after he had embraced and kissed her.

"I've been refighting the battles of Crécy and Agincourt—"

"Crécy and Agincourt! Did the Prince of Wales inspire you to do that?" he stared at her abdomen.

She laughed. "No, I haven't felt a move all week. He—or she—must be sleeping."

"Then why are you thinking about Crécy and Agincourt?" He frowned.

"We won the Battle of Crécy because of the longbow. Right?"

"Your Majesty, you are right."

"Since the French knew that, why didn't they use longbows at Agincourt sixty-nine years later?"

"I—I really don't know."

"Could it be that there is an ancient weapon even older and more effective than the longbow which we might use to help civilize the world?" She pulled the drape open and musingly looked out the window.

"I—I don't really know. Nimrod in the Old Testament must have used a bow and arrow."

"I've been thinking about the weapons Jesus mentioned in His sermon on the Mount—"

"For example?"

"Jesus said, 'But I say unto you, That ye resist not evil: but whosoever shall smite thee on thy right cheek, turn to him the other also' " (Matt. 5:39).

"Oh, oh, but—"

"And didn't the Apostle Paul say, 'Therefore if thine enemy hunger, feed him; if he thirst, give him drink: for in so doing thou shalt heap coals of fire on his head'?" (Rom. 12:20).

"But, but, but—"

"Isn't the Word of God stronger than the longbow or the crossbow or modern gunpowder?"

"It is. But, but—but you must remember the reason we won at Crécy is because His Majesty Edward III was present to inspire the men—and because his sixteen-year-old son, the Black Prince, also fought by his side. And that fact also explains Agincourt. His Majesty Henry V was also present in that battle. He stayed in the thick of the fight and fought with his royal helmet on his head.

"Albert! I've been honored by providence! And I'm going to use my position to help make the world better."

"And how are you going to do that?" Albert assumed an extrawise look.

"It's true that I'm merely a figurehead," explained Victoria. "My speeches are written by others. I have to sign documents whether I agree with them or not. My suggestions may not even be considered. But I do have certain powers. I can set prisoners free. I can confer titles. If I choose, I could honor a beggar with a baronetcy."

"And when will Your Majesty make your mother a dowager?" he teased.

"Probably never," Victoria teased back. She thrust out her diminutive chin. "But I am going to encourage everyone who does right. And I'm going to set a good example. Being the Defender of the Faith means something to me."

Victoria continued to have false labor. But early on the morning of November 9, she began to feel sharp birth pangs. Summoning her nurse, she said, "I think you'd better alert Doctor Locock."

Locock puffed in just in time to deliver a healthy boy at twelve minutes past eleven. The Archbishop didn't arrive until after the Queen gave the potential Prince of Wales his first lunch. Nonetheless, there was no controversy over the gen-

uineness of his birth. He was duly christened Albert Edward
in St. George's Chapel.

Edward and Vicky were a few days less than eleven and a
half months apart.

That December, Albert introduced a new idea to Great
Britain. He ordered a number of Christmas trees from Coburg. Much to the dismay of Victoria and the servants, he
decorated the trees with colorful trinkets, artificial stars and
candles. Thus, he introduced the Christmas tree to Great
Britain.

The heavy snow during Christmas week brought playfulness to the Queen. Albert made her a twelve-foot snowman.
He played games with her and pushed her sled across the ice.

That winter, Albert continued streamlining the bureaucracy at both Buckingham and Windsor. By slashing expend-
itures and increasing efficiency, he managed to save tens of
thousands of pounds. He also got rid of the brass instruments that formed a large part of the orchestra that played
during their meals. Stringed instruments were more to his
taste. He especially liked chorales and the music of Bach and
Martin Luther.

On the 30th of May, he accompanied the Queen on a trip
to the mall. As they rode near a large mass of people, Albert's
eyes were suddenly drawn to "a little swarthy ill-looking rascal." He had barely noticed him, when, from a distance of
only two paces from the carriage, the little man whipped out
a pistol, took careful aim at the Queen, and pulled the trigger.

The gun failed to fire. The would-be assassin disappeared
into the throng.

On the following afternoon, Victoria said, "I'm sure he'll
try again, so let's return and give the police a chance to catch
him."

Albert looked at her in surprise. "But Your Majesty, he
may kill both of us. He's undoubtedly practicing right now."

Victoria laughed. "Don't worry. We've already produced
two heirs. If one isn't crowned Edward VII, the other will be
crowned Victoria II!"

Unable to even force a smile, Albert commented, "Your Majesty, you sound rather foolhardy."

"I'm not foolhardy. God has a task for me to do. He has shown me the weapon I'm to use. His providence will continue to protect me."

As the hour of their departure to the mall approached, a lady-in-waiting prepared to accompany her. "No, you'd better stay here," ordered the Queen. "There is no need for you to risk *your* life."

"How about the men?" argued the Lady.

"Oh, it's their job to risk their lives protecting me. And so that's perfectly all right."

Again, the "ill-looking rascal" whipped out a pistol, took deliberate aim and pulled the trigger from about five paces away. The bullet went under the carriage. Victoria heard the report of the gun, but remained perfectly calm. The police instantly captured the assailant.

John Francis was tried and condemned to death, much to the regret of the Queen. Later, due to a technicality, the death penalty was reversed and he was merely deported for life.

Perhaps encouraged by the light penalty inflicted on John Francis, John William Bean, a four-foot dwarf, decided that it was now his turn to attempt to assassinate Her Majesty. On July 3, he sneaked up to her and fired his pistol. Fortunately he had loaded it with only paper, tobacco and a small amount of gunpowder. No harm was done.

Sir Robert Peel, having heard about the attempt, rushed to Buckingham Palace. When he found the Queen in good spirits, he burst into tears.

The battle between Lehzen and Albert continued. Victoria tried to be a catalyst in order to enable them to endure one another. As she prayed about the matter, the eyes of the Empire focused on the Opium War in China.

The war ended with the Treaty of Nanking, signed on HMS *Cornwallis* on August 29, 1842. In order to dramatize their contempt for the agreement, the Chinese appended their signatures without formally reading it.

The agreement opened up trade to the British, allowed them access to five ports and forced the Chinese to pay them a huge indemnity over a period of three years. The Chinese guaranteed their payments by agreeing they would turn over to the British Chou-shan and a small island dominating Amoy if they did not keep up their payments. Opium was not mentioned in the treaty.

On April 25, Victoria gave birth to her second daughter. Writing about the event three weeks later, she informed King Leopold:

> Our little baby, who I am really proud of, for she is so very forward for her age, is to be called Alice, an old English name, and the other names are to be Maud (another old English name and the same as Matilda) and Mary, as she was born on Aunt Gloucester's birthday.[1]

Victoria's happiness, however, was marred by Albert's insistence that Lehzen be retired. Eventually, Victoria gave in. But she softened the blow by presenting the Baroness with a carriage and by arranging for her to receive an annual pension of eight hundred pounds.

Lehzen moved in with a sister who lived in Bukeburg in northwest Germany. Unfortunately, her sister died two months later. But, being a minor celebrity, Lehzen got along well. To those who viewed her photographs and questioned her about the Queen, she invariably answered, "I never saw such a passionate and naughty child as Victoria. But I never knew her to tell a falsehood, even though it meant she would be punished."

---

[1]*Queen Victoria in Her Letters and Journals,* 1985, p. 95.

15

The Crystal Palace

As calenders turned to 1849, Queen Victoria had many reasons to be happy. Britain had remained at peace with her neighbors since the defeat of Napoleon in 1815. The Corn Laws had been repealed in 1846. (These laws, sneered at as "hunger taxes" by the poor, had been enacted to support the price of grain. They accomplished this by taxing grain imports. A side effect of the law raised the price of food beyond the buying power of many.) In addition, she had given birth to three more children. Alfred made his appearance in 1844, Helena in 1846 and Louis in 1848. Moreover, all six of her children were in reasonably good health. Besides these blessings, the United Kingdom remained the most prosperous nation in the world.

Yet Victoria had a major problem that gnawed at her soul day and night. Her beloved Albert had not been generally accepted by the aristocracy. Those in power, together with those with inherited titles and vast estates, did not like his German accent. Nor did they appreciate his lack of enthusiasm for polo and other aristocratic recreations.

As Victoria prayed and sometimes wept over the matter, she realized the aristocratic attitude could only be changed by a miracle. Nonetheless, she believed in miracles, for she had seen a miracle take place right before her eyes. That miracle was the transformation of the political beliefs of Sir Robert Peel.

Peel, founder of the London police force, was a popular man. They called the police "bobbies" in honor of his nickname. Born to wealth, he became a Tory member of Parliament when only twenty-one. In that position, he defended the rich. In addition, when he became Prime Minister in 1841, he promised he would not seek to repeal the Corn Laws.

As the rich became richer because of those laws, famine gripped Ireland and many in England faced starvation. These facts opened his eyes. Much to the consternation of the rich, he became a Whig and lashed out against the Corn Laws, managing to get them repealed.

Peel's conversion to Whig principles and free-trade was almost as miraculous as the conversion of Saul on his way to Damascus. *Could such a conversion change the attitude of the aristocracy toward Albert?* Victoria sincerely hoped so.

Incredibly, one of the elements that helped transform public opinion had its beginnings in a strange water lily a British traveler had seen in Guiana. Impressed by its enormous size, he took some of its seeds back to England and presented them to Kew Gardens. There, the resulting plants were carefully cultivated. None grew to significant size.

Then Joseph Paxton, a self-trained architect, secured a cutting and planted it in a heated tank at Chatsworth. The heat apparently did not help. He then placed some paddle wheels in the water to keep it circulating.

The lily needed the churning water. Like Jack's beanstalk, it headed for the sky. Within three months it had eleven leaves, each five feet across. In addition, there grew enormous blooms. Paxton presented his prize to Queen Victoria and named it Victoria Regia.

Victoria Regia continued to grow. While viewing it, Paxton impulsively placed his little girl on one of the leaves. To his profound amazement, he discovered her weight did not even bend the leaf. Carefully studying the underside of the leaf, he learned the strong radiating ribs were strengthened by cross ribs. Staring wide-eyed, he came to the conclusion that he had discovered a source of strength that might become as useful as the Roman Arch.

He used what he learned to build a conservatory.

While Paxton enjoyed the lily and its house, a committee planned a huge building four times the size of St. Paul's to house a proposed exposition. Several plans were submitted, none satisfactory. Learning this, Paxton approached the Building Committee, asking if he could submit a design.

"Time is very short," replied the chairman, tapping the desk with a ruler. "But if you could submit a plan within a week or two, we'll consider it."

Challenged, Paxton worked day and night. Using the principle of the water lily, he completed his plan in nine days. The building he envisioned would be built of glass and tubular steel, containing 33,000,000 cubic feet of space. His idea had many advantages, including the fact that it would be cheap to build and could easily be dismantled.

The committee was impressed.

Extremely sensitive to art, Prince Albert became the President of the Society of Arts in 1847. In this position, he had played a leading role in planning three small expositions which displayed British art and manufacture. Having had this experience, a Royal Commission formed in 1850 with Prince Albert as president.

The idea of an extremely large exposition continued to expand in the manner of Paxton's water lily. At first it would be the largest. Then it would not only be the largest but it would also be the first *international* exposition—one in which all nations would be invited to participate. Albert bubbled with enthusiasm. "It will spread knowledge around the world," he assured the Queen.

Victoria shared his enthusiasm, even though she expected another baby in the spring. Melting in his arms, she murmured, "I'm so proud of you. One task of the British Empire is to spread knowledge around the world."

A debate ensued on where the building should be erected. Prince Albert suggested Leicester Square. Another member argued for Hyde Park. Eventually, the Royal Commission chose Hyde Park.

That decision became as a red flag to a bull. It infuriated the public. Horrified clergymen denounced the idea in blistering sermons. Pounding their pulpits, they declared the international exposition would be like another Tower of Babel; it would summon God's wrath on their heads.

Medical men joined in the denunciation. They assured the public the international scope of the exposition would usher in a new siege of the bubonic plague, killing tens of thousands, maybe even hundreds of thousands.

As wave after wave of invective swept the nation, Victoria and Albert's new baby made his appearance on May 1. Christened Arthur, he was later named the Duke of Connaught. Arthur, a healthy child, sat in the number three spot in the lineup as heir to the British Throne.

In June, *The Times* erupted with a series of blasts at the proposed *International Exposition*. Victoria's face tensed as she read, "The whole of Hyde Park and the whole of Kensington Gardens will be turned into a bivouac of all the vagabonds of London."

"What do you think of that?" asked the Queen as she handed the paper to Albert.

Albert forced a smile. "Humanity has always been against progress. Always!"

"Aren't you worried?" She paused with her knitting.

"No. Why should I be? The Lord showed us how to build the exposition building by designing the Guiana water lily and inspiring Joseph Paxton to discover its secret of strength. The *International Exposition* will inspire all of mankind!"

The newspapers never tired of ridiculing Albert's project. Soon members in the House of Commons had their turn. One outspoken critic was Colonel Sibthorp, an eccentric MP from Lincoln.

Sibthorp seemed to be against anything that was not quite within his horizons. Being a Protestant, he stormed against Catholic Emancipation. Hating railways, he fought the Railway Bill. He marched against the Library Act because he didn't like to read. He enjoyed being an opposer.

Sibthorp became quite disturbed because some trees in Hyde Park were being cut to make room for the *International Exposition*. He stood in the House of Commons and asked a sneering question. "Are the elms to be sacrificed for one of the greatest frauds, greatest humbugs, greatest absurdities ever known?"

Sibthorp's opposition ignited additional opposition. Even while the newspapers blackened with contempt and the House churned with name-calling, Queen Victoria had other troubles.

During the last week of June, while Sir Robert Peel rode up Constitution Hill, his horse slipped and fell on him. Two days later, as he struggled with a broken rib in his lung, someone struck Victoria over the head with a cane. Fortunately, the rim of her hat softened the blow.

The next day, Prime Minister Peel passed away. A grief-stricken Victoria prayed:

> Oh! God Who alone knows what is best for us, may thy will be done, but it does seem mysterious that in these troubled times when *he* could less be spared than any human being, he should be taken from us.[1]

Wearily, Queen Victoria rose from her knees. She walked to the window and watched the setting sun. Watching pastel colors paint the sky, she was convinced that in spite of her troubles, she was still a providential queen, assigned by God to special tasks. She thought back on the attack of the previous day. To the Queen, her escape was simply proof that a guardian angel had been watching over her. It was the same angel who had watched over her the month before when a man had fired a blank cartridge at her.

That evening, at the Royal Opera, a five-minute standing

---

[1]*Queen Victoria, Born to Succeed*, 1964, p. 219.

ovation lifted her sagging spirits.

Concentrating on the exhibition, Albert kept busy in spite of the constant ridicule aimed at him by the press. No one at the time had ever used glass for building purposes. The wise ones were confident that a hailstorm would ruin the nearly one million square feet of glass. Albert maintained his confidence.

The steel ribs—like those in the water lily—were raised within a week. Some of the building encompassed entire trees. As the amazing building mushroomed within a few months, Sibthorp continued exercising his vocal chords in the House of Commons. "Who will pay for it?" he stormed. "The foreigner? Why he has no money. The House has been told the laborers throughout the country will save their shillings that they might be enabled to visit the exhibition. Who will take care of their families whilst they are away from London? What will become of the chastity and the modesty of those who might become unsuspecting victims of those temptations?"[2]

Ignoring the critics, the engineers and their 2,000 workers kept busy. In one week they installed more than 18,000 panes of glass. They built eleven miles of stalls with enough room to display 100,000 exhibits.

As the structure neared completion, a totally unexpected calamity developed.

Fleeing from the cold park, hundreds of sparrows invaded the glass shelter, built nests in the trees, rested on the steel ribs, laid eggs and bombed those beneath them.

Paxton and his friends discussed the problem by the hour. Guns could not be used. Poison was not permissible. No one had a solution.

They approached the Queen for her suggestion. Victoria pondered for a brief moment. Then she replied, "I don't have *the* solution. But I believe there is one man who can solve the

---

[2]*The Crystal Palace*, 1970, p. 22.

problem. "Who?" demanded the spokesman, forgetting about protocol.

"The Duke of Wellington!"

Hours later, the victor of Waterloo approached the throne.

"And what should they do?" asked the Queen.

Wellington smiled as he bowed low. "Your Majesty," he replied, "let them try sparrow-hawks."

Queen Victoria laughed, as did everyone else.

After devouring the sparrows, the hawks searched for their dinners elsewhere.

Fourteen thousand exhibitors from countless nations arranged exhibits in the waiting stalls. By the end of April, London was alive with foreign visitors. Hotels jammed. Every capable vehicle overflowed with passengers. Newspapers printed articles in many languages. Money flowed. Everyone was happy with the exception of Sibthorp and his followers.

The exhibits included arts of every description: paintings, statues, carvings, jewels, clocks, saddles, ivory thrones, lace, fine linens, pottery, porcelain, etc.

Mechanical devices lured the curious with miniature bridges, locks, ships, railway layouts, lighthouses and even canals.

Birmingham displayed an array of handcuffs, shackles, leg irons and fetters that had been created to sell to the slave States in America.

The medical section was especially attractive with exhibitions of new inventions to aid doctors. One device substituted for leeches when a patient needed to be bled. Also displayed were artificial legs and arms and various noses made of silver.

The American display included milk-churns, a piano that could be played by four pianists at the same time, the model of a floating church and a vacuum coffin that guaranteed the body placed in it would never decay.

On opening day, a throng of thirty thousand waited patiently for the Queen and Prince Albert to arrive. After they entered and sat on the dais, the Archbishop of Canterbury offered a public prayer. Then a great organ led a choir in singing the Hallelujah chorus.

Forgetting their previous negative stance, *The Times* reached for superlatives:

> There was yesterday witnessed a sight the like of which has never happened before. . . . They who were so fortunate to see it hardly knew which to most admire. . . . Some saw in it the second and more glorious inauguration of their Sovereign; some a solemn dedication of art and its stores; some were most reminded of that day when all ages and climes shall be gathered round the Throne of their Maker.[3]

Victoria's joy at the success and public acclaim of her Albert lifted her spirits as high as they had ever been. In her journal on May 1, 1851, she wrote:

> This is one of the greatest and most glorious days of our lives, with which, to my pride and joy the name of my dearly beloved Albert is forever associated! It is a day which makes my heart swell with thankfulness. . . . God bless my dearest Albert, and my dear Country which has shown itself so great today. . . . Everyone was astounded and delighted. . . . Dearest Albert's name is forever immortalized and the absurd reports of dangers of every kind and sort . . . are silenced.[4]

Deep within her heart, Victoria determined she would confer upon her husband the title *Prince Consort*. But, as the result of experience, she realized that the time for the honor must wait for the future.

---

[3]Ibid., p. 42.
[4]*Queen Victoria in Her Letters and Journals*, 1985, pp. 84–85.

16
Crimea

Both Victoria and Albert eventually tired of Buckingham Palace, Windsor Castle and even Brighton. Having adequate income, the Queen longed to have a place outside London where she and Albert could be alone with their children. "I get so sick of London with its cement, chimneys and fogs, I feel like a bird in a cage," complained Victoria.

Victoria and Albert rented an 800-acre estate on the Isle of Wight in 1844 and immediately fell in love with the place. The next year they purchased it. The existing house was too small, so they had a mansion built and moved into it in 1846. They also purchased an additional fifteen hundred acres, naming the estate Osborne. Here, with woods and valleys and a private beach, Victoria and the Prince were extremely happy. By planning their activities, they managed to go there four times a year for complete relaxation.

All of the children had a job at Osborne. Each had a tool with an initial written on it and each worked under a foreman who was encouraged to criticize their work. It was difficult for him to say, "Prince Edward, I think you missed some weeds," or, "Princess Victoria, you must dig a little deeper and make your rows straight." But he managed.

The children received the same wages as other servants. In addition to cutting lawns, cultivating gardens and sweeping drives, the girls, who were old enough, were required to prepare a dish for the table each day.

In the early part of 1853, while she carried her eighth child, Victoria received a copy of the American bestseller, *Uncle Tom's Cabin* written by Harriet Beecher Stowe. Both she and Albert were entranced by the book. One day Victoria stopped reading. Looking over the top of the novel, she said, "Albert, I want you to listen to this." She explained that Simon Legree had been standing by a group of slaves he had just purchased, and was chatting with a stranger. Her voice breaking, she read:

> . . . Now, you see, I just put 'em straight through, sick or well. When one nigger's dead, I buy another; and I find it comes cheaper and easier, every way.

After blowing her nose, Victoria asked, "And what do you think of that?"

Albert hung his head. "I'm remembering those handcuffs and leg irons we displayed at the Exposition. A lot of them were made for the American slave-trade. We may have even made those that were used on Uncle Tom." He shuddered.

"That sort of thing bothers me," responded the Queen, laying the book on the tea table. "But Albert, we *are* doing something about it. We stopped the Trade in 1807; and in 1834 we paid twenty million pounds to the planters in Jamaica to free their slaves. Also, remember, when slaves reach Canada, they are free."

"True, but we should use our navy to stop other countries from dealing in slaves. Right now, even while I speak, slaves are still being sold in Zanzibar."

"That is so. But you know, there is a Scottish missionary doctor in South Africa who is doing something about it. His name is David Livingstone. He went out during the Opium War."

Albert nodded his head. "Certainly. I've heard of him. The Secretary of State for Foreign Affairs is always corresponding with him, isn't he?"

"Yes. Livingstone is convinced that if the Zambezi River

can be navigated, it will be the key to opening Africa for trade, missionary work and for stanching the slave-trade."

"How could it stop slavery?" Albert asked.

"Simple. If the natives can earn money by selling us cotton, why should they raid their neighbors to sell their children into slavery?"

In the spring of 1853, as Victoria approached the day she would deliver her eighth child, Doctor Clark called to check on her. This birth concerned him because she neared her thirty-fourth birthday.

As he removed his stethoscope from his stovepipe hat, he said, "Your Majesty, you have an excellent opportunity to help medical science."

"In what way?"

"Six years ago, Doctor Snow from Edinburgh, gave a doctor's wife chloroform when he delivered her baby. Since it eased the pain, she named the baby Anaesthesia. Now, if it's all right with Your Majesty, I'd like to invite Doctor Snow to give you some chloroform when I deliver your baby."

"How will that help medical science?" Victoria asked.

"Your Majesty, the masses have great faith in you because of your exemplary life. If you allow us to give you chloroform, others will not be afraid to use it and thousands will be blessed." The doctor sighed and replaced his stethoscope. "There has been a lot of argument over the use of chloroform during childbirth."

"Why?" Victoria frowned.

"Those against it quote Genesis 1:16, '. . . in sorrow they shall bring forth children . . .' Those for it, stand on Genesis 2:21, 'And the Lord caused a deep sleep to fall upon Adam and he slept: and he took one of his ribs, and closed up the flesh thereof.' "

Victoria laughed. "I like the idea of the deep sleep," she said.

"And so do I," agreed the doctor.

The Queen went into labor on April 7, delivering a boy

who was duly christened Leopold George Duncan Albert.

The Queen wrote about the chloroform:

> [Doctor Snow] gave that blessed Chloroform & the effect
> was soothing, quieting & delightful beyond measure.

Unfortunately, the new baby Prince Albert was rather delicate. The diagnosis of hemophilia came later.

Victoria and Albert loved their palace on the Isle of Wight, but after their first visits to Scotland in the late 40's, their hearts were at Balmoral. There, in the Highlands, close to Braemar, they purchased an estate that eventually covered 30,000 acres. For the Royal family, it was an ideal place. They enjoyed the forests, the valleys, the rivers, the salmon, the game and the people.

They appreciated living among the Highlanders. Victoria especially appreciated not being addressed in royal terms.

In 1853, Albert designed a magnificent castle and called in an Aberdeen architect to oversee the work. He included in the design a large ballroom where Victoria could enjoy herself in her favorite pastime—dancing. The children enjoyed all the room. Victoria attended services at a nearby kirk with the servants and neighbors.

In her book, *Our Life in the Highlands*, which Victoria wrote and published in 1868, she included a paragraph about the church she and Albert attended.

> We went to Kirk as usual at twelve o'clock. The service
> was performed by the Rev. Norman McLeod, of Glasgow, son
> of Dr. McLeod, and anything finer I never heard. The sermon, entirely extempore, was quite admirable; so simple,
> and so eloquent, and so beautifully argued and put. The text
> was from the account of the coming of Nicodemus to Christ
> by night; St. John, chapter 3. Mr. McLeod showed in the
> sermon how we all tried to please self, and live for that, and
> in so doing found no rest. Christ had come not only to die
> for us, but to show how we are to live. The second prayer
> was very touching; his allusions to us were so simple, saying, after his mention of us, "bless their children." It gave
> me a lump in my throat, as also when he prayed for the

"dying, the wounded, the widow, and the orphans." Every one came back delighted; and how satisfactory it is to come back from church with such feelings! The servants and the Highlanders—all—were equally delighted.[1]

Victoria also enjoyed visiting the poor.

> Mrs. P. Farquharson . . . walked around with us to some of the cottages to show me where the poor people lived, and to tell them who I was. Before we went into any we met an old woman who . . . was very poor, eighty-eight years old, and the mother of the former distiller. I gave her a warm petticoat, and the tears rolled down her old cheeks, and she shook my hands, and prayed God to bless me; it was very touching.
>
> I went into a small cabin of old Kitty Kear's, who is eighty-six years old—quite erect, and who welcomed us with a great air of dignity. She sat down and spun. I gave her also a warm petticoat; she said, "May the Lord ever attend ye and yours, here and hereafter; may the Lord be a guide to ye, and keep ye from all harm . . ."[2]

The Queen herself got a spinning wheel and spent many an hour relaxing as she spun both cotton and wool. In her castle, she was like a light on a hill. She established a lending library for the neighbors, and specialized in visiting the elderly, many of whom could not quite comprehend that she was the Queen of the world's largest empire. But Victoria's days of relaxation were soon ended by the ominous stirrings that began to erupt between Turkey and Russia.

For centuries, Russia had been envious of Constantinople. Waiting for an excuse to attack this ancient city which controlled the Black Sea, the Russians bided their time. The time came in the dispute over who should control the keys to the Holy Sepulchre in Jerusalem.

The French insisted the keys belonged to the Catholic church. Since Turkey controlled Jerusalem, Russia and Turkey were soon glaring at one another. And, since Napoleon had warned: "If Russia should hold the Dardenelles, she would be at the gates of Toulon, of Naples, and Corfu," France

---

[1]*Our Life in the Highlands*, Queen Victoria, pp. 70–71.
[2]Ibid., pp. 81–82.

was eager to help the Turks keep Russia from occupying the Dardenelles.

As tension mounted, war-fever in Britain zoomed. The average person wanted to side with France. But Prime Minister Aberdeen vehemently opposed such an alliance. Both Victoria and Albert agreed with the Prime Minister. Nonetheless, Home Secretary Palmerston outmaneuvered him.

The masses retaliated by circulating a rumor that Prince Albert was a traitor, and would be sent to the Tower. And so firmly was this believed, crowds lingered at the gates expecting to see him thrust inside.

Responding to pressure, British ships sailed for Turkey in February, 1854; and on March 27 and 28, Britain and France formally declared war on Russia.

The Crimean War, dreaded by both Victoria and Albert had become a reality. The Royal Family was heartsick.

Of that useless conflict, one battle stands out: The Charge of the Light Brigade at Balaclava.

The war had concentrated in the Crimean Peninsula—a large piece of land extending into the Black Sea. Near the tip of this peninsula on the western side lay the port of Balaclava. Having occupied this city, the British decided to move northwestward and attack Sebastopol less than ten miles away.

Since a plan of Sebastopol's fortifications had been discovered, the British felt confident they could take the port without much difficulty.

When Lord Raglan studied the area through a telescope, it appeared the British "Heavies" had been successful; the Russian cavalry was retreating and taking their cannon with them. Convinced he faced a great opportunity, he spat out an order, written by an unknown hand on a scrap of blue paper. Badly scribbled in pencil, it read:

> Lord Raglan wishes the cavalry to advance rapidly to the front, and try to prevent the enemy from carrying away the guns. Troop of Horse Artillery may accompany. French Cavalry is on your left. Immediate, R. Airey

The Light Brigade, an army of 673 confident men charged

up the valley to capture the Russian guns. They soon discovered those guns were in position to fire on them, with cannons on either side. The plumed men clothed in red had ridden into the jaws of death. Only 200 returned. The remaining 473 men were killed along with 475 horses.

The mistaken order had resulted in one of the bloodiest defeats in British history. After studying the facts, Alfred Tennyson was inspired to write:

> "Forward the Light Brigade! Charge for the guns," he said:
> Into the valley of Death Rode the six hundred.
> Theirs is not to reason why,
> Theirs but to do and die:
> Into the valley of Death Rode the six hundred.

Many read those lines and mourned their dead. Yet when Florence Nightingale read them, she thought of some facts that Tennyson did not know. This lady who gave up wealth to become a nurse wrote to influential friends about things she witnessed while she tried to save men's lives. Ink flowed from her pen like blood from the many wounds:

"At the hospital there are no clean shirts . . . The men have only rags saturated with blood . . . The hospital has been transformed from a barrack . . . and underneath its imposing mass are sewers loaded with filth, through which the wind blows fetid air up the pipes into the wards where the sick men are lying . . . the wards are infested with rats, mice and vermin. . . . The vermin might, if they had unity of purpose, carry off the four miles of bedding on their backs and march with them into the War Office in London. . . .

"The iron beds from London arrived at Scutari, but the legs for the beds were put on another ship and sent on to Balaclava. The sick and wounded at Scutari lie on mattresses on the stone floors."

Victoria's eyes dampened as she read the letters from Florence Nightingale. When praised for inspiring a new generation of greats, the Queen prayed additional opportunities would come her way, opportunities which would enable her to prove to the world the power of God's truth, which was far older and stronger than the longbows used at Crécy and Agincourt.

When she checked her engagement calender, she noticed she would be paying a state visit to Paris that summer. Perhaps Paris would bring her the opportunities she so desired.

17

The Widow at Windsor

W hile war raged in Crimea, Queen Victoria kept busy signing documents, consulting her ministers—and exchanging
visits with heads of state. On August 18, 1855, she, along
with Albert and their two eldest children, boarded the *Victoria and Albert* yacht at Cowes and sailed for Boulogne.

No English sovereign had paid a state visit to France since
the one-year-old English King, Henry VI had been crowned
King of France 433 years before.

Napoleon III met the Royal family at Boulogne. The en-
thusiastic welcome at the docks dazzled Victoria. As she and
her family drove through the crowded streets to the Palace of
St. Cloud, the masses kept shouting *"Vive la Reine d' An-
gleterre! Vive l'Empereur! Vive le Prince Albert!"*

From there they traveled to Paris by train.

The highlight of the Queen's journey to the French capital
was her visit to the Hotel des Invalides, the site of Napoleon's
tomb. Reliving the solemn occasion, she wrote:

> There I stood, on the arm of Napoleon III, his nephew,
> before the coffin of England's bitterest foe; I, the grand-
> daughter of that King who hated him most, and who most
> vigorously opposed him, and this very nephew who bears
> his name, being my nearest and dearest ally! The organ of
> the church was playing "God save the Queen" at the time,
> and this solemn scene took place by torchlight, and during

a thunderstorm. Strange and wonderful indeed![1]

The Queen, as she viewed the marble tomb beneath the circular rail, thought of the battles of Morengo, Austerlitz, Trafalgar, Borodino, Waterloo. She remembered how Napoleon seized the crown from the Pope's hands and placed it on his own head. She also remembered the words of Jesus: ". . . but whosoever shall smite thee on thy right cheek, turn to him the other also" (Matt.5:39).

Turning to her fourteen-year-old son Edward she said, "Kneel at the foot of Napoleon's tomb." Edward immediately obeyed, and as he did so, many of the French generals began to weep. They had witnessed the humanly impossible.

In an incredibly dramatic manner, Queen Victoria had demonstrated that biblical weapons are more powerful than human weapons. And she underlined that truth before the entire world in an unmistakable way. For centuries, England and France had been at one another's throats, but from that unbelievable moment in the Hotel des Invalides, they've remained at peace with one another.

The Crimean War continued, and so did the efforts of Florence Nightingale. At first she remained respectfully silent, hindered by the blundering incompetents who dominated her. Then shortly after her arrival at Scutari, 27,000 shirts arrived and the shivering men could not wear them until a key official gave permission. A determination to ignore red tape gripped her. Her jaw set, she knew what to do when the next shipment of shirts arrived. "Open the packages and distribute the shirts," she directed.

At the beginning of the conflict, nearly one half of the wounded died, but as a result of her work only two out of a hundred died.

As hostilities continued, the armies faced a new problem. Cholera and typhus haunted the camps. Thousands perished, but neither Florence Nightingale nor any of her nurses

---

[1] *Victoria R.*, 1959, p. 56.

gave up. They ignored personal time schedules. Twelve and often twenty hours of duty each day became normal.

Queen Victoria became inspired by her efforts, and she responded by reading, listening, praying—and working. She kept her knitting needles busy and mailed scarfs and mittens to the front. She also wrote personal letters to bereaved mothers and widows.

After three days of bombardment, Sebastopol fell to the French on September 8, 1855. This overwhelming victory over the Russians ended most of the fighting. But the treaty ending the war was not signed until March 30, 1856. That document had cost more than half a million lives.

Even though an agreement had been reached, the monks in Jerusalem continued to fight over the keys of the Holy Sepulcher.

The end of hostilities, however, did not stop Queen Victoria's commitment. Realizing wounds needed to heal and positive values should be acquired from the disaster, she continued working toward that goal. In January, even before the treaty was signed, she wrote to Florence Nightingale:

> You are, I know, well aware of the high sense I entertain of the Christian devotion which you have displayed in this great and bloody war, and I need hardly repeat to you how warm my admiration is for your services, which are fully equal to those of my dear and brave soldiers, whose sufferings you have had the privilege of alleviating in so merciful a manner. With this letter, I send a broach, the form and emblems which commemorate your great and blessed work, and which, I hope, you will wear as a mark of the high approbation of your Sovereign![2]

In the form of a badge, this broach featured the Cross of St. George in crimson enamel. The Queen's name was topped by a crown of diamonds, and the words "Blessed are the merciful" circled the entire broach.

Queen Victoria took special interest in each soldier she visited. She often picked up the bullet or bit of shrapnel which had been removed from the victim's body and de-

---

[2]*Queen Victoria in Her Letters and Journals*, 1985, p. 135.

scribed it in her journal. Thus personally experienced with some of the problems the soldiers had faced, she arranged for Florence Nightingale to visit her at Balmoral.

During one of their conversations, Florence related how a certain Corporal Courtney had taken to drink after having a bullet removed from his eye. She then suggested the Queen's influence could help keep such men "straight."

Challenged to use her influence, the Queen visited the incorrigibles in various hospitals. Prince Albert frequently suggested certain ones were impossible, but the Queen never shared his feelings. Moreover, many who had been given up by others, received new hope when "touched" by the Queen.

The Queen's highly respected touch caused a minor problem. Many times after she had pinned a medal on a veteran, the honored man was reluctant to have his name inscribed on it for fear it might be exchanged for a duplicate which the Queen had *not* touched.

After the fall of Sebastopol, Victoria and Albert relaxed at Balmoral. Both assumed the years ahead would be bright with tranquility. They were mistaken. In retrospect, the storms of the past were minor squalls in comparison to the series of typhoons just ahead.

Even before workers began clearing debris from the burned city, Victoria and Albert's eldest daughter had fallen in love with a German prince. Fritz, the nickname of Prince Frederick William, was the son of the heir to the Prussian throne. At the age of fourteen, Vicky felt convinced that Fritz was the greatest man who had ever lived, and Fritz, ten years her elder, joyously returned Vicky's heartfelt love and affection.

Fritz received permission from the Queen to pay special attention to Vicky. Not long afterward, the two young lovers were engaged, with the restriction of waiting to marry until Vicky turned seventeen. Ecstatic over her daughter's happiness, Victoria recorded her feelings in her journal:

> He [Fritz] kissed her hand twice, I kissed him and when
> he kissed her hand again . . . she threw herself into his

arms, and kissed him with a warmth which was responded to by Fritz again and again and I would not for the world have missed so touching and beautiful a sight . . . it is first love! Vicky's great youth makes it even more striking, but she behaved as a little girl of 18 . . ."[3]

Delighted with her daughter's forthcoming marriage, Victoria spent many happy hours assisting with the wedding details. Still, she had numerous private concerns, as she was once again pregnant. The doctors had assured her that her new baby, the ninth child, would be due in early spring—and they were right. Beatrice was born on April 14, 1857.

During her convalescence, Victoria decided she had waited long enough to convey another title on Albert. Most of those who had despised Albert were either dead or out of office, and after checking with Prime Minister Palmerston, the Queen made her announcement. She bestowed upon Albert the title Prince Consort—the same title that had been conferred upon Queen Anne's husband. *The Times* shrugged at the honor, but the vast majority of her subjects felt Albert had more than earned his title.

On January 25, 1858, Victoria watched with pride as Vicky dressed for her wedding. The Honiton lace of the gown and the bridal veil reminded Victoria of her own wedding so many years ago. She felt happy that Vicky's marriage would be one filled with love, just as hers had been. With this wedding though, there was one major annoyance. Hundreds of the grooms relatives descended on London. She had to keep many of them in Buckingham Palace. Their enormous moustaches with twisted horns on the ends were bad enough. What sickened her most was that a few of them completely ignored her NO SMOKING signs. Both she and Albert so hated tobacco, they had posted similar signs in all their official residences.

Vicky soon became pregnant, and at full-term, went into labor at Potsdam early in the morning of January 26, 1859. Queen Victoria worried over the labor, because Vicky's preg-

---

[3]*Queen Victoria*, 1921, pp. 369–370.

nancy had been most difficult. Victoria assigned her own physician, Doctor Martin, to help. As the British doctor rolled up his sleeves, one of the German doctors remarked in English, "It's no use. The Princess and her baby are dying."

Dr. Martin remained undisturbed even though he knew Vicky had overheard the remark. He simply continued his work. With great skill and by the use of chloroform, he eventually delivered the baby even though it was a breech presentation. Both mother and prince survived. But, sadly, due either to nerve damage during pregnancy, or to an injury sustained during the difficult birth, the Prince's left arm dangled at his side, out of the socket and extremely blue. It would remain withered and useless the rest of his life.

They christened the infant Frederick William Albert Victor. Victoria frowned when she learned her grandson had forty-two godparents. Nonetheless, she beamed with pride over her new title no Parliament could ever bestow—that of grandmother.

From the time Queen Victoria had read Uncle Tom's Cabin and seen the handcuffs and leg irons sold to American slavers, she had been intensely interested in the animosity growing between the Northern and Southern states in America. Each issue of *The Times* bannered a more alarming headline than the previous issue.

"Listen to this," said Victoria as she rested her cup of tea on the table. She read from *The Times*, "In the recent election, President Lincoln did not carry a single Southern state and South Carolina has already seceded from the Union."

Albert stared. "I'm afraid a war between the North and South is inevitable."

"If there is such a war—and God forbid—I hope we stay out of it."

In the following weeks, more sensational news darkened the papers. Within six weeks an additional six states had united with South Carolina giving birth to the Confederacy.

As the war clouds in America gathered, Victoria's attention turned to a more personal problem. Prince Consort Albert succumbed to the pressures of overwork. In February, he was confined to his room with a swollen jaw.

Doctors operated twice on his gums, but the surgery provided little relief. Summoning all the strength he possessed, he wrote in his diary: "My sufferings are frightful, and the swelling will not come to a proper head."

Victoria stayed by his side as much as her schedule would allow, and gradually he was able to get up and wander about the apartment. Then another devastating blow sent them to their knees. Victoria's mother became dangerously ill. Since her first attack of erysipelas (St. Anthony's fire) in 1859, the seventy-five-year-old Duchess had become increasingly helpless. On March 9, 1861, her right arm was so swollen she had to undergo surgery. But the surgery did not help. Then with almost unbearable pain, her left arm began to swell also.

When Albert went to see her a week later, she was in so much pain he burst into tears. Thoroughly alarmed, Victoria rushed to her mother's side. The Queen recorded in her journal the agony that both mother and daughter felt:

> Oh! what agony and despair was this! . . . I knelt before her, kissed her dear hand and placed it next to my cheek; but though she opened her eyes, she did not, I think, know me. She brushed my hand off, and the dreadful reality was before me, that for the first time she did not know the child she had received with such tender smiles! I went out to sob. . . . I asked the doctors if there was no hope. They said, they feared none. . . . As the night wore on into the morning, I lay down on the sofa, at the foot of my bed. . . . I heard each hour strike. . . . Albert took me out of the room for a short while, but I could not remain. . . . I sat on a footstool, holding her dear hand. . . . I felt the end was fast approaching, as Clark went out to call Albert. . . . Fainter and fainter grew the breathing. At last it ceased. . . .The clock struck half-past nine at that very moment.[4]

This was the first personal death Queen Victoria had experienced. She took it so hard that Albert and others feared her sanity. For three weeks she insisted on eating alone. She bared her heart in her journal: "It is dreadful, dreadful to

---

[4]Ibid., pp. 417–418.

think we shall never see that kind loving face again, never to hear that voice again . . ."

As the Queen's grief continued unabated, some began to secretly wonder if she had inherited the instability which had affected her grandfather, uncles, and many distant relatives. Albert did all he could to comfort her, but he was unable to help. Then his attention turned to another important matter.

On April 14, 1861, the Confederates fired on Fort Sumter, setting in motion war between the Union and Confederate armies.

That fall, the Confederates commissioned John Slidell to go to France and James Mason to go to England to secure recognition for the Confederacy; and perhaps even arrange for some financial backing. Both gentlemen decided to cross the Atlantic together.

The Union forces had blockaded Southern ports. The gentlemen, realizing the hazard of trying to get by the guarding cruisers, decided to hire the *Gordon*, a privateer, to take them to Havana. There they boarded the British mail ship *Trent* and sailed for England.

The *Trent* had not gone far when Americans stopped and boarded it. Both Mason and Slidell were arrested. This action broke International Law. In so doing, they twisted the British lion's tail. The British lion responded with a mighty roar. Soon 8,000 British troops headed for Canada.

Each side had strong feelings. The Americans remembered the British had burned the White House in 1812. The British smarted because the embargo hurt their trade with the Confederacy. The Americans said Mason and Slidell were worse than Benedict Arnold. A large section of the House of Commons wanted to dismember the American republic.

The war of words was an invitation for satirical poems. *Harper's Weekly* came out with a parody of *God Save the Queen*:

> God save me, great John Bull!
> Long keep my pockets full!
> Great John Bull!
> Ever victorious,

Haughty, vainglorious,
Snobbish, censorious,
Great John Bull!

Even though Seward, the American Secretary of War, had threatened to "wrap the whole world in flames," those with perspective realized the problem would have to be solved peacefully. The Union simply could not afford to go to war against Britain, or even have Britain be officially sympathetic with the Confederacy.

The war of words needed to be quenched.

As the Trent affair sputtered into flame, Albert became very ill. His diary reveals he was full of "rheumatic pains," and he had "scarcely closed his eye for the last fortnight." While he struggled with his undiagnosed illness, he kept thinking about the Trent affair and a possible solution.

From Victoria he learned the cabinet believed "a gross outrage" had been committed, and that Her Majesty's Government had a right to "demand" complete satisfaction.

While the Queen entertained guests at Windsor, Prince Consort Albert received copies of letters to the British Ambassador in Washington. And so while Victoria chatted with William Gladstone and other celebrities, Albert forced himself to study those documents.

As he read the wording, he shuddered. Some of the sentences seemed harsh, unyielding. He still remembered how the French Generals had wept when his son knelt before the tomb of Napoleon, and he remembered that Solomon had said, "A soft answer turneth away wrath: but grievous words stir up anger" (Prov. 15:1).

With these ideas in mind, he wondered if he might discover a way to save face for both sides and thus avoid a head-on collision.

Although his fever continued to soar, he worked and prayed at the same time. Thoughtfully, he mentioned the "friendly relations which have long persisted between Great Britain and the United States." He also stated Her Majesty's Government was willing to believe the captain of the American ship had acted on his own. He further indicated that after the release of the "captives," Britain would be in a position to accept an apology.

By the time Albert had completed his changes, he was exhausted. It took all the willpower he could summon to remain at the desk.

Queen Victoria read the document at breakfast. "You did an excellent job," she said, as she signed it with a flourish.

The crisis teetered for several additional weeks during which Britain prepared for war. Then uncanny providence overshadowed the problem. The often unreliable Atlantic cable broke down, and thus provided a cooling off period. Eventually Albert's modified message was received and accepted. The crisis was over.

Albert and his physicians hoped his illness was temporary, but he continued to deteriorate. They summoned Doctor Jenner, an expert who had worked at the Fever Hospital. Even he was baffled, and nothing he did helped. Occasionally, the sometimes delirious patient improved. Then he would be convulsed with coughing fits. He refused to stay in bed. As he wandered from room to room, he often did strange things. Once he asked Princess Alice for music; and so a piano was wheeled into his room and she played his favorite hymn, *A Mighty Fortress Is Our God*. On another occasion he knelt by the Queen and called her "Gutes Weibchen" (excellent little wife). Frequently, he asked someone to read to him or to hold his hand.

By the morning of December 14, it was clear that unless the Lord intervened, he would not live through the day. At about 9:39, while the sun streamed through the window, Princess Alice sorrowfully remarked that she could hear "the death rattle."

Hurrying to his bed, Victoria knelt and murmured, "Es ist Kleiness Frauchen" (It is your little wife). She held his hand and requested a kiss. He responded feebly, and minutes later he was gone.

Victoria, halfway through her 41st year, realized that millions depended upon her for courage, and she momentarily contained her grief. When at last the funeral services were

*

over and she was at Windsor Castle and apart from the throngs, she plunged into the excessive and prolonged mourning that continued the rest of her life. It was this unrelenting mourning that inspired many to refer to her as that *Widow at Windsor.*

18

Empress of India

Dressed severely in black, Queen Victoria stood before the tall living room window at Windsor Castle and stared outside. Wherever she gazed she saw the monotonous blankness of snow. The grounds were white, the trees were white, the driveways were white, the chimneys were white, the roofs were white. The white emptiness stretched in all directions and reminded her of her own emptiness.

For six weeks following the Prince Consort's death, she tried to sleep with his pajamas in her arms and his picture on the pillow next to hers. But his picture and pajamas remained empty. They had no breath, no warmth, no life. They all but mocked her. *The Lord had sent Albert to comfort and strengthen her. Why, oh why, did He have to take him away?*

She closed her eyes and tried to weep. The comfort of tears would help, but they refused to come. She had already wept far too much. Without realizing it, she began to repeat the words of Jeremiah: "Oh that my head were waters, and mine eyes a fountain of tears, that I might weep day and night . . ." (9:1).

During the succeeding months of agony, Victoria continued to relive some of the peak moments of the past. One that shifted into sharp focus concerned the way she and

Albert had promoted the creation of the *Victoria Cross*. After a long discussion with Albert, the Queen suggested each awardee be called B.V.C. (Bearer of Victoria Cross). Both of them agreed it should be awarded for valor in the presence of the enemy, that its holder should receive an annual income of ten pounds—and that it should be awarded to all classes in the armed forces, both in the Army and Navy.

Reliving the past was like enjoying a fresh breeze on a hot day, and the Queen frequently lost herself in her memories. Still, her grief continued. Lord Herford came for a visit and was troubled by what he saw. He pictured Her Majesty as "the most desolate and unhappy of God's creatures but one gifted by Him with a strength of mind . . . seldom if ever granted to a woman."[1]

People all over the Empire sympathized with the Queen, and each day thousands offered prayers in her behalf. Victoria sought relief in any legitimate thought with a possibility of finding comfort. She became especially interested in immortality. *Would she live again? And if she did, would she and Albert recognize one another?*

With such questions haunting her mind, she put on a disguise and went to the Metropolitan Tabernacle to hear Charles Spurgeon, the young Baptist whose sermons were stirring the entire city. She also dipped into every religious book she could find, particularly those which dealt with life everlasting. On a top shelf she found *In Memorium*, a book composed of several poems by Lord Alfred Tennyson. Leafing through it, she discovered he had been inspired to compose these lines as the result of the death of his friend Arthur Henry Hallman.

Admiring Tennyson because of his *Charge of the Light Brigade*, the Queen eagerly took the volume into her room. Soon, her heart began to lift as she identified with the theme and especially certain lines. She read and reread:

The great world's altar-stairs,

---

[1]*Queen Victoria, Born to Succeed*, 1964, p. 312.

That slope through darkness up to God.

Having studied the stars with Albert by her side, she understood those lines. Other lines also flicked bits of hope. One couplet especially intrigued her, for on many a dark day she had wrestled with doubts—primarily about immortality. After reading them silently numerous times, she dramatized them out loud:

> There lives more faith in honest doubt, Believe me, than in half the creeds.

Encouraged by *In Memorium*, Queen Victoria invited Tennyson to visit her at Osborne. Oddly dressed and with dark flowing hair and a full beard, Victoria received him with appreciation. Together, they discussed various parts of *In Memorium* and the heartbreak caused by death.

Although helped by his comments, the Queen felt a persistent vacuum in her heart. Feeling a need for spiritual strength, she attended St. Paul's and worshiped with the regular congregation. Both the music and the sermon were inspiring, only now a new question tormented her. *Assuming immortality was a fact, was there any way in which she could be assured she would personally live forever?* She searched her heart. She knew she was morally pure, and she had never told a lie. Ah, but there were other problems. She had been harsh with her mother and she had even spoken sharply to Albert. Deeply concerned, she decided to consult her chaplain.

"Is there any way in which I can be assured I will go to heaven?" she asked.

"No, Your Majesty, there is not," he replied as he nervously adjusted his clerical collar.

"What am I to do for complete assurance?"

"Just believe, and hope, and have faith. God is merciful . . ."

Troubled, Victoria often lingered by the tall windows at Windsor and watched the trees swaying in the breeze. One day, as she considered her need for assurance, she felt a strange confidence that it would be forthcoming.

Through an unexplained means, the story of the Queen's conversation with the chaplain came to the attention of an obscure minister by the name of John Townsend. Feeling a strong compulsion, Townsend addressed a letter to the Queen and outlined for her the way of assured salvation. He wrote:

"The Bible says, 'For God so loved the world, that he gave his only begotten Son, that whosoever believeth in him should not perish, but have everlasting life' (John 3:16)."

He then went on to insist ". . . all have sinned and fallen short of the glory of God" (Romans 3:23). Next, he clinched his point by quoting Rom. 10:9: "If thou shalt confess with thy mouth the Lord Jesus, and shalt believe in thine heart that God hath raised him from the dead, thou shalt be saved."

The Queen read his letter, checked the scripture passages in her Bible, and then replied that she now "believed in the finished work of Christ for me." She also said she would be looking forward to meeting him in heaven.[2]

Gradually, Queen Victoria began to spend more time in Balmoral. Her attachment to the Scottish Highlands grew with the years. She loved the swirl of bagpipes, the kilts, the rushing burns, the nearby sea, the mist from the white tails of the waterfalls and the clatter of kettles on the hob in the stone houses of her neighbors. She loved the sheep on the hillsides, the heather, the salmon, and the sudden leap of the deer. She also reveled in the lack of protocol. She didn't even wince when her servant John Brown addressed her as "woman" and didn't bow.

Victoria loved the local kirk, and when the pastor delivered a sermon she especially liked, she requested a copy and mailed additional copies to her closest friends.

When she needed to be in London, she made the forty-eight-hour journey in a special luxury train coach built for that purpose. It came equipped with a comfortable bed, a

---

[2]See tract titled *Blessed Assurance*, published by Good News Publishers.

desk, a living room, and special compartments for her servants. While traveling, she dined from gold plates just as at home.

Often, as the wheels click-clacked over the rails on her way home to Balmoral, the past flashed before her in vivid colors. Memories of Albert never faded. They were as real as the black mourning garments she insisted on wearing.

Years before, when she first announced her engagement to the Privy Council, she had worn a bracelet, with a miniature picture of Albert attached to it. She still wore it. She retained a picture of Albert on the pillow next to her own and kept several paintings of him on the various walls. Her favorite painting featured him in a field marshal's uniform. In addition to the photos and paintings, she always kept a marble bust of him nearby.

Just after Albert's death, Victoria wrote in her journal: "The things of this world are of no interest to the Queen . . . her thoughts are fixed above."

Now, as the train whistle sounded at a crossing, a new thought glimmered in her mind. From experience, she had learned blind people develop unusual gifts to help compensate their loss of sight. *Could it be that even though she had lost Albert, the Lord would make up for him in some other way?* Praying and thinking about the matter, she felt assured that He would do just that.

The train continued on its way, and Victoria's memories moved on to her coronation. She remembered the joy she had experienced when she helped Lord Rolle regain his dignity, kneel at her feet and extend his homage. She never could forget the tears that filled the old man's eyes and the thunderous acclaim she received after she had extended her hand to him.

That joy, she knew, came to her because she had obeyed the Lord in helping an unfortunate brother. Gradually, the train slowed for its stop. After Victoria settled back into her beloved Balmoral, she began to think about David Livingstone, the young Scot, who had gone to Africa as a missionary during the Opium War. Across the years, Lord Clarendon had kept her informed about his activities.

Livingstone believed God had called him to be a pathfinder in order to enable missionaries and traders to penetrate into the depths of the continent. When Livingstone wanted to explore the mighty Zambezi river, Lord Clarendon had consulted with Victoria, then addressed a letter to "Our esteemed Friend Sekeletu, Chief of the Makololo, in South Africa." On February 19, 1858, he wrote:

> Ours is a great and commercial and Christian nation, and we desire to live in peace with all men. We are all children of one common Father; and the slave-trade being hateful to him, give you proof of our desire to promote your prosperity by joining you in the attempt to open up your country to peaceful commerce. This is "God's pathway . . ."[3]

Through casual comments by Lord Clarendon, the Queen continued to receive haunting glimpses of Livingstone's career. From the security of her palace, she had followed him as he explored the broad Zambezi, sought the source of the Nile, and visited the Zanzibar slave-market where he vowed he would fight the "cursed trade" as long as he had breath.

Eyes overflowing and memories of Albert flooding her heart, the Queen identified with Livingstone as he sat by the crude bedside of his dying wife in Shupanga. Fascinated with this incredible Scot who had turned his back on the luxuries offered by an adoring public in order to follow the leadership of the Lord, Victoria persisted in her quest for knowledge about the man. She read all his books and followed Henry Morton Stanley's story in the papers which told how he had "found" Livingstone at Ujiji in 1871.

Stanley's book, *How I Found Livingstone*, sharpened the Queen's interest in the man. She, along with the entire world, felt shocked at the news of his death in Chitambo's village on May 1, 1873.

---

[3]*Personal Life of David Livingstone*, 1881, p. 488.

Divine providence seemed at work once again. On May 1, the very day Livingstone died, the British Government began negotiations with Sultan Barghash of Zanzibar in order to persuade him to close all his ports to the slave-trade. Threatened by a blockade if he did not comply, he signed the treaty on June 5th, and on that same day, the slave-market in Zanzibar closed forever.

Queen Victoria's name was known and respected all over the world. Through the British East India Company, Britain had indirectly ruled India since the latter part of the 1700s. After a rebellion with Indian soldiers in 1857, Britain decided India would be ruled by the British Parliament, and not by The East India Company which had a tendency to be cruel.

British India—the new name—came into reality in 1858. As Victoria studied the situation, she concluded that British Rule, even during The East India Company years, had been beneficial to the Indians. This was especially true when she thought about the suppression of *suttee*—the burning of live widows on their husband's funeral pyres—as ordered by Parliament in 1829.

Victoria was vitally concerned about the manner in which British India would be ruled. Eventually, a proclamation, partially shaped by her influence, was issued. It read:

> . . . Firmly relying ourselves on the truth of Christianity . . . we disclaim alike the right and desire to impose our convictions on any of your subjects . . . all shall enjoy the equal and impartial protection of the law.

Although happy with the progress Britain made in India, the Queen felt troubled by one seemingly insignificant thing. She summoned her secretary, Sir Henry Onsonby, in January, 1873, and said, "I am Empress and in common conversation am sometimes called Empress of India. Why have I never assumed this title? I feel I ought to do so, and wish to have preliminary enquiries made."

Victoria's request was examined, and after some be-hind-the-hand-smiles, Prime Minister Benjamin Disraeli introduced a bill which would award the Queen that title. With only token opposition, Victoria was officially declared Empress of India on May 1, 1876. The proclamation was repeated in Delhi by the Viceroy, Lord Lytton, on January 1, 1877. The Rajah of Travancore, indicating his approval, presented her with an elaborate ivory throne.

19

The Final Years

With her children gone and the grandchildren growing up in distant cities, Queen Victoria often felt depressed. The emptiness of great palaces and the ho-hum grind of day-in-day-out monotonous routine had a way of convincing her she had been nothing but a parasite. Experience, however, had taught her the best way to fight depression was through prayer, reading the Bible—and activity.

Victoria dipped her quill and wrote to each of her off-spring. This was a heavy task, for, in addition to her nine children, she had thirty-eight grandchildren. Also, she had to keep up with their ever-changing titles. This was not easy. In the beginning, a note to Vicky required the formal address: Crown Princess of Prussia. After 1888 this had to be changed to Empress Frederick of Germany. Later, when Vicky's eldest son came to the throne after the one-hundred-day rule of his father, Frederick III, her letters to him had to be addressed: Kaiser Wilhelm II.

In addition to the therapy of writing letters, Victoria had the joy of harvesting some of the products from the good deeds she had sown. In a morning paper in the summer of 1867, she read:

> Prior to his death on August 25, our reporter interviewed the famous scientist, Michael Faraday. "What are your spec-

ulations of life after death?" he inquired. "Speculations!" cried the seventy-six-year-old developer of the dynamo, "I know nothing about speculations. I'm resting on certainties. 'I know my Redeemer liveth,' and because He lives I shall live."

Mulling that over, Victoria remembered how after she had learned Michael Faraday and his wife Sarah were having a hard time reaching their attic apartment, she had offered them a rent-free house in Hampton Court. After looking it over, Michael shook his head. "We can't take it, for we don't have the necessary funds for repairs." She then paid for the renovations herself, and the Faradays moved in.

After studying Faraday's statement about immortality again, Victoria's mind went back to the time Albert had held her hand and assured her they would be together in the next life. Faraday's statement had underlined Albert's words, and they had firmed her own assurance. This extra assurance had more than repaid her for all the expense and trouble.

Queen Victoria still loved to read and none of the five and six hundred page novels of the period were too long. She especially liked Charles Dickens, Sir Walter Scott, and George MacDonald, the Scottish writer who specialized in poetry and novels with a Christian motif.

After learning of MacDonald's poverty, Victoria had arranged for him to receive an annual pension of one hundred pounds. Her encouragement enabled him to write many more books. Books that later inspired such giants as C. S. Lewis.

Strangely, Victoria's obsession to use biblical weapons to advance the cause of the British Empire frequently advanced causes in which she had no particular interest. An example is the bettering of the plight of the poor. When Victoria first became Queen, the middle-class was extremely small. Her subjects were either rich or very rich; poor, or exceedingly poor. There were some with incomes of five thousand pounds a day, and others with incomes of five pounds a year.

Having visited a gypsy encampment, Victoria felt deeply moved by their poverty. Yet when she approached Prime Minister Melbourne, she learned his attitude was "let's not upset things." Nonetheless, the moral Christian life which she practiced had its effect—especially on such people as Anthony Ashley-Cooper, later the Seventh Earl of Shaftesbury.

Nineteenth century England had been sickened by black slavery, for the masses had seen—and smelled—slave ships awaiting repairs. Yet the same masses had become indifferent to the child slavery that churned in their midst. Yes, they had seen soot-drenched five- and six-year-olds with their shaved heads and stovepipe hats; and they heard them shout, "Sweep! Sweep! Sweep!" as they solicited trade. They also knew many of these little boys died early because of soot cancer. Nevertheless, Britain merely shrugged or mumbled, "How shocking."

England was not unusually hardhearted. The trouble was the children did not have a spokesman. But God had not overlooked them. In due course, Lord Shaftesbury, won to Christ by his governess Maria Millis and inspired by John Wesley and Charles Spurgeon, became their spokesman.

On August 4, 1840, a tired House of Commons yawned when Shaftesbury stood to make a motion. A busy day, scant attendance, and boring speakers had drained everyone. As he began, he knew he might be interrupted by those who wished to adjourn. He silently prayed God would give the House patience to hear him out.

His motion concerned the employment "of children of the lower classes in the mines . . . and various branches of the trade . . ."

When he began to hurl statistics, the MPs settled down. He spoke of seven-year-olds working twelve hours a day in tobacco factories, of youngsters working eighteen hours a day in the knitting mills and of the horrors children endured in the coal mines.

He concluded by paraphrasing the sentiments for which Queen Victoria stood. "I may be charged with cant and hypocrisy. . . . But I must regard [the children] as being created, like ourselves, by the same master, redeemed by the same Savior, and destined to the same immortality."

The MPs proposed a bill that faced horrendous opposition. Mine owners fumed it would ruin industry. Nonetheless, public opinion supported the bill. On August 8, Shaftesbury scribbled in his diary, "Took sacrament on Sunday in joyful and humble thanksgiving to Almighty God, for the undeserved measure of success with which He has blessed my effort for the glory of His name . . ."

Two days later the bill was law.

As time passed, it seemed to Victoria each year vanished sooner than the previous one. She continued to pause by a window and relive her yesteryears—especially those with Albert. Sometimes Baroness Lehzen also came to mind. After Lehzen had retired to Germany, she occasionally heard from her. In the late sixties Victoria learned Lehzen had fractured her hip. Distraught, she immediately sent her a wheelchair. Then, while visiting Paris in 1870, a telegram announced Lehzen had passed away on September 9.

Lehzen's last words were "Victoria, Victoria . . ."

Victoria wept. In a letter to Vicky weeks later, she commented, "I owed her much and she adored me."

After the death of Poet Laureate, Lord Alfred Tennyson in 1892, literary people wondered whom Her Majesty would appoint to fill the vacancy. Almost everyone assumed it would be Rudyard Kipling. This man, born in India, was the most popular writer in England. His *Barrack Room Ballads*, which included the rhythmic *Gunga Din*, was a current sensation. Moreover, he accepted and pushed the Victorian dogma that it was England's sacred duty to civilize the world.

In spite of what the masses wanted, Queen Victoria extended the honor to the unimaginative Alfred Austin. The strongly suspected reason for this is that a Kipling poem, *The Widow at Windsor*, canceled his chances forever. It included the following quatrains:

> 'Ave you 'eard o' the Widow at Windsor
> With a hairy gold crown on 'er 'ead?
> She 'as ships on the foam—she 'as millions at 'ome
> An' she pays us poor beggars in red.
>
> Walk wide o' the Widow at Windsor,
> For 'alf o' Creation she owns:

> We 'ave brought 'er the same with the sword an' the flame,
> An' we've salted it down with our bones.

On September 23, 1896, having passed the record set by her grandfather George III, Victoria became the longest reigning monarch in British history. The next year, during the Klondike Gold Rush, she celebrated her Diamond Jubilee. Six years before that, she had written, "May God enable me to become worthier, less full of weakness and failings, and may He preserve me for some years." Now, in her 78th year, she still hoped to be around for a few more years.

During the magnificent celebration which commemorated her fifty-year reign, Queen Victoria, still wearing black, awarded titles, reduced prison terms, encouraged missionaries—and received accolades from all over the British Empire, and other parts of the world. The elderly often commented about the changes they had witnessed during her reign.

At the time of Victoria's birth, it was impossible for a Jew, Catholic, or Dissenter to obtain a degree at any English University. That era was now gone. Benjamin Disraeli, son of Isaac Disraeli, was born a Jew, and yet on two occasions served as Prime Minister during Victoria's reign.

In Victoria's childhood, England was dominated by agriculture. Now it was thoroughly industrialized. The factories had produced problems, but the problems were dealt with in a series of bills that eventually struggled into law. These included the Friendly Societies Act, the Public Health Acts, and the Factory Acts.

During Victoria's reign, the standard of living improved. The national income tripled, artisans were given annual holidays, water and gas were piped into homes throughout the nation, steamboats crossed the oceans, a web of railways speeded transportation throughout Britain, advances were made in medicine, and more people were allowed to vote.

In addition, the British Empire became the largest empire the world had ever known. It had grown by one third during Victoria's reign. The telephone had been invented and a moving picture was made of her. One invention she didn't like was the electric light. Squinting at one, she complained, "It hurts my eyes."

Some new laws annoyed her, especially the "death tax." This levy, she feared, would cripple the aristocracy. She was also horrified by the suggestion women be allowed to vote. Indeed, she felt so strongly on the subject that she suggested the leader who had promoted the idea should be "horse-whipped."

The Boer War in 1899 created a dark year for Victoria. All went well for the Boers (Dutch farmers who had migrated to South Africa) until gold was discovered in the Transvaal—the land beyond the River Vaal. That discovery was a magnet for thousands, many of them British. Soon, clashes between the Boers and the gold-seekers flamed into the Boer War.

Britain rushed troops to the area, but the Boers, knowing the country, had one success after another. Deeply concerned, Victoria followed the action with intense interest, though her eyes had become so dim even the telegram had to be read by an assistant.

By 1900, as a result of additional troops, the British began to win the war. Victoria rejoiced in each success and lamented every setback. By November she was so tired and worn-out she noted in her journal, "My appetite is completely gone and I have great difficulty in eating anything."

In spite of her failing health, she forced herself to remain at her desk. On the last day of November even though it was cold, she inspected some Canadian troops, and had personal words of sympathy for the wounded who managed to reach her carriage. On December 18, she moved from Windsor to Osborne. A paragraph which she dictated for her journal indicates the condition of her health:

> I had a bad night though I got a little sleep at the beginning. Besides, I don't think I could have slept, as there was such a fearful storm. Then I thought of what would be going on. . . . The weather was so tempestuous that I got quite alarmed about it. I went to sleep again, after I had wished to get up. . . . It rained and blew so hard that it was impos-

sible to think of going out, so I did some signing, though I could hardly see a word I wrote.[1]

The Queen's health continued to slide downward. Her journal for January 1, 1901, contained this line, "Another year begun and I am feeling so weak and unwell that I enter upon it sadly."

Despite her despondency, she forced herself to send her regular New Year's greeting to her Prime Minister, Lord Salisbury. He must have wept when he read the almost illegible sentence, *"The Old Year dies; God beckons those we love."* The signature was a mere splotch. But he knew it stood for Victoria, Regina, India.

By the 17th, the Queen began to have mental troubles. Even so, at times she was completely rational. Bulletins kept the world alert as to her condition. And from all over the world, heads of state sent messages indicating their concern. A remarkable one was received from Paul Kruger, a leader of the Boers in their fight against the British. He stated his interest in her "prompt recovery."

The Queen did not get better. By the 22nd, those around her knew that her life would end soon. Archbishop Davidson and the local Vicar of Whippingham were summoned, and both of them periodically prayed for her. She made no move to indicate she was even aware of their presence. Baffled, the clergymen exchanged glances. Then Davidson began to quote one of the Queen's favorite hymns—Cardinal Newman's *Lead, Kindly Light.* As he reached the final part of the last verse, he suddenly became aware that she was listening. Having waited to be with Albert for forty years, the Queen especially cherished the concluding lines:

> And with the morn those angel faces smile, Which I have loved since, and lost awhile.

The Prince of Wales and Kaiser Wilhelm remained with the crowd of children and grandchildren who surrounded the bed. The Kaiser kept supporting her pillow with his right arm. But since his left arm was withered, it was impossible

---

[1] *Victoria the Widow and Her Son*, 1934, p. 378.

for him to rest by moving to the opposite side.

As those in the room waited, Davidson noticed the tenseness in the Queen's face suddenly vanished and was replaced by a look of "complete calmness." At 6:30 in the evening of January 22, 1901, Victoria took her last breath. The earthly journey of the Providential Queen and Defender of the Faith had finished its course.

Epilogue

Knowing the Lord planned to summon her, Queen Victoria prepared her will. Its preamble indicated her readiness for promotion, and it conveyed where she wanted to be buried.

> I die in peace with all fully aware of my many faults, relying with confidence on the love, mercy and goodness of my Heavenly Father and His Blessed Son and earnestly trusting to be reunited to my beloved Husband, my dearest Mother, my beloved Children and three dear sons-in-law. And all who have been very near and dear to me on earth.
>
> Also I hope to meet those who have so faithfully and so devotedly served me especially good John Brown and good Annie MacDonald who I trusted would help lay my remains in the coffin and to see me placed next to my dearly loved Husband in the Mausoleum at Frogmore.

Two additional items must be noted about the Queen's instructions. 1. Her coffin was to be transported on a gun-carriage. This was to honor her father who was a military man. 2. She insisted that her body be dressed in white. The reason is obvious. Her dark period of mourning had passed. She had reached the divinely appointed time for coronation, and the meeting of loved ones.

In that Victoria had instructed undertakers not be used, the Kaiser measured her body and arranged for the coffin. Likewise, he insisted the Union Jack be displayed at Osborne

House where her coffin lay in state for ten days.

On February 1, the coffin was placed on the royal yacht *Alberta*. It made the crossing by sailing between eleven miles of battleships and cruisers. The day was gray and sunless as if the entire world mourned. As the Alberta passed each naval ship, it responded by firing a salute. The black cannon smoke added to the drama. German and French battleships also anchored nearby. The French had not forgotten Trafalgar nor Waterloo, but neither had they forgotten that the "Queen of the Seas" had ordered her eldest son, now King Edward VII, to kneel before the tomb of Napoleon Bonaparte.

When the sealed train bearing the coffin puffed into Windsor station, the horses attached to the gun-carriage became nervous. Therefore, they were unharnessed, and the gun-carriage was pulled up the steep incline to the candle-lit St. George's Chapel by a team of naval bluejackets. Following a brief funeral service, the coffin moved on to Albert Memorial Chapel. It remained there during the night, surrounded by flowers from heads of state who wanted to honor Europe's "Grandmama."

At a private service the next day, only the Royal family followed the coffin to the nearby Frogmore mausoleum where Victoria's remains were placed next to those of Albert.

Victoria's passing was honored by speeches, telegrams, flowers, and gun-salutes. Two of the most significant honors, however, came from unexpected quarters. Upon hearing of her death, a Zulu chief pointed to the sky and exclaimed, "Then a new star has been flung unto the heavens." And in Dublin, a newsboy added a handful of violets to the poster which announced the Queen's death.

Upon her passing, Queen Victoria had been reigning sixty-three years and seven months and was nearly halfway through her eighty-first year.

Chronology

1714		Queen Anne, the last of the Stuarts, died.
		George I, first of the Hanoverians, became king.
1727		George II, son of George I, crowned.
1760		George III, grandson of George II, inherited the throne.
1776		American Colonies declared freedom.
1819	May 24	Victoria was born to the Duke and Duchess of Kent.
	Aug. 26	Albert was born to Duchess Louise of Saxe-Coburg.
1820	Jan. 23	Duke of Kent died of pneumonia.
	Jan. 29	George IV followed his father George III as king.
1824		Lehzen became Victoria's governess.
1830		William followed his brother George IV to the throne.
	Mar. 11	Victoria discovered she might become Queen.
1831		William IV tries to change Victoria's name.
1835	July 30	Victoria confirmed.
		Victoria's favorite text became, "Behold, now is the day of salvation" (2 Cor. 6:2).
		Gossip circulated that the Duchess of Kent was too fond of Sir John Conroy, her comptroller.
	Oct. 31	Victoria had a severe case of typhoid.
1837	June 21	Victoria proclaimed Queen.
		Insists mother move into her own room.
		Victoria dismisses Conroy.
1838	June 28	Victoria coronated.

1840	Feb. 19	Victoria and Albert married.
	June 12	Victoria survived first assassination attempt.
	Nov. 22	Victoria, Princess Royal, born.
	Dec. 8	David Livingstone sailed for Africa.
		Opium War with China flames into reality.
1841	Nov. 9	Edward, Prince of Wales, born.
1842	May	Queen escapes second assassination attempt.
	July	Queen escapes third assassination attempt.
	Aug.	Defeated China signed "unequal rights treaty."
1843	Apr. 25	Second daughter, Alice, born.
		Lehzen retired under pressure from Albert.
1844	Aug. 8	Second son, Alfred, born.
1846		Albert made additions to Osborne, their new mansion.
	May	Third daughter, Helena, born.
1847		Queen and Albert leased Balmoral, a house in Scotland.
1848	Mar. 18	Louise, fourth daughter, born.
1849	July	Victoria survived fourth assassination attempt.
	Aug.	Queen donated twenty-five guineas to David Livingstone for discovering Lake Ngami.
1850	May 1	Arthur, third son, born.
	June	Queen escaped fifth assassination attempt.
1851	Apr. 7	Queen popularized chloroform by using it during the birth of Leopold, her fourth son.
		Outbreak of Crimean War.
1855	Aug.	Visited tomb of Napoleon Bonaparte.
1857	Apr. 14	Beatrice, fifth daughter, and last child, born.
	June 25	Albert given title of Prince Consort.
1861	Dec. 1	Albert softened letter in the "Trent Affair."
	Dec. 14	Albert died of typhoid. Victoria was then 42 and had reigned 24 years.
1872		Queen escaped sixth assassination attempt.
1876	May 1	Queen Victoria declared Empress of India.
1882	Mar. 2	Queen escaped seventh assassination attempt.
1897	June 20	Queen celebrated Diamond Jubilee.
1898	May 19	Death of William Gladstone.
1899		Boer War broke out.
1900	Apr. 4	Assassin attempted to kill the Prince of Wales.
	Jul. 30	Alfred, Victoria's second son, died.
1901	Jan. 22	Queen Victoria died at Osborne at 6:30 P.M.
		Prince of Wales was named King Edward VII.
	Feb. 4	Victoria's remains were placed in the mausoleum next to those of Albert.
1902		Boer War concluded.

Queen Victoria's Prime Ministers

ELECTED

April, 1835	Viscount Melbourne
September, 1841	Sir Robert Peel
July, 1846	Lord John Russell
February, 1852	Earl of Derby
December, 1852	Earl of Aberdeen
February, 1855	Lord Palmerston
February, 1858	Earl of Derby
June, 1859	Lord Palmerston
November, 1865	Earl Russell
July, 1866	Earl of Derby
February, 1868	Benjamin Disraeli
December, 1868	W. E. Gladstone
February, 1874	Benjamin Disraeli
April, 1880	W. E. Gladstone
June, 1885	Marquis of Salisbury
February, 1886	W. E. Gladstone
August, 1886	Marquis of Salisbury
August, 1892	W. E. Gladstone
March, 1894	Earl of Rosebury
July, 1895—July, 1902	Marquis of Salisbury

Bibliography

Algernon, Cecil. *Queen Victoria and Her Prime Ministers*. Eyre & Spottiswoode, 1953.

Aspinall, A., *Letters of Princess Charlotte*. Home and Van Thall, 1949.

Auchincloss, Louis. *Persons of Consequence, Queen Victoria and Her Circle*. Random House, 1979.

Barker, A.J. *The Vainglorious War, 1854–56*. Weidenfeld and Nicolson, 1970.

Barlow, Frank. *Edward the Confessor*. University of California Press, 1970.

Beaver, Patrick. *The Crystal Palace*. Hugh Evelyn, Ltd., 1970.

Beeching, Jack. *The Chinese Opium Wars*. Hutchinson & Co., 1975.

Bennett, Daphne. *VICKY, Princess Royal of England & German Empress*. St. Martin's, 1971.

Blaikie, Wm. J. *Personal Life of David Livingstone*. Harper, 1881.

Bolitho, Hector. *The Reign of Queen Victoria*. Macmillan, 1948.

———. *Victoria, the Widow and Her Son*. Appleton, 1934.

Boykin, Edward. *Victoria & Albert and Mrs. Stevenson*. Rhinehart, 1957.

Briggs, Asa. *Victorian People*. University of Chicago Press, 1955.

Brook-Hunt, Violet. *The Story of Westminster Abbey*. James Nisbet & Co., 1904.

Brown, Beatrice Curtis. *The Letters of Queen Anne*. Funk and Wagnalls, 1935.

Campbell, R.J. *Livingstone*. Ernest Benn, Ltd., 1929.

Cecil, David. *Melbourne*. Bobbs-Merrill, 1939.

Chancellor, Beresford. *The Regency Rakes*. Philip Allan & Co., 1925.

Clark, Ronald W. *Balmoral, Queen Victoria Highland Home*. Thames and Hudson, 1981.

Clarke, John. *The Life and Times of George III*. Book Club Associates, 1972.

Colston-Baynes, Dorothy. *The Youthful Queen Victoria*. Putnam, 1952.

Coupland, Sir Reginald. *Livingstone's Last Journey*. Collins, 1945.

Duff, David. *Victoria and Albert*. Taplinger, 1892.

Durant, Will. *The Story of Civilization, Part XI*. Simon and Schuster, 1975.

Ferris, Norman. *The Trent Affair*. University of Tennessee Press, 1977.

Finlayson, Geoffrey. *The Seventh Earl of Shaftesbury*. Eyre Methuen, 1981.

Flint, John. *Cecil Rhodes*. Little Brown, 1974.

Frazer, Antonia. *Cromwell, The Lord Protector*. Knopf.

Fulford, Roger. *George the Fourth*. Duckworth, 1935.

Gibbs, Peter. *Crimean Blunder*. Holt, Rhinehart and Winston, 1960.

Gernsheim, Helmut and Allison. *Victoria R*. Putnam, 1959.

Gopal, S. *British Policy in India, 1858–1905*. Cambridge, 1965.

Graeme, Bruce. *A Century of Buckingham Palace*. Hutchinson & Co., 1937.

Gregg, Edward. *Queen Anne*. Routledge & Kegan Paul, 1980.

Greville, Charles. *Greville Memoirs of George IV and William IV*. Longman Green and Co., 1874.

Hibbert, Christopher, *Greville's England*. Folio Society, 1981.

———. *Queen Victoria in Her Letters and Journals*. Viking, 1985.

Hibbert, Christopher. *George IV, Prince of Wales*. Harper and Row, 1972.

Holt, Edgar. *The Opium Wars in China*. Putnam, 1964.

James, Lawrence. *Crimea and the War With Russia*. Hayes Kennedy, 1981.

Johnson, Paul. *Elizabeth I, a Study in Power and Intellect*. Weidenfeld and Nicholson, 1974.

Jones, William. *Crowns and Coronations*. Chatto and Windus, 1902.

Kronenberger, Louis., *The Great World, Portraits and Scenes from Greville's Memoirs*. Doubleday, 1963.

Kumar, Ajit Ray. *Widows Are Not for Burning*. ABC Publishing House, 1985.

Lofts, Nora. *Anne Boleyn*. Coward McCann & Geoghegan, 1987.

Longford, Elizabeth. *Queen Victoria, Born to Succeed.* Harper and Row, 1964.

Lichtervelde, Comte Louis de. *Leopold First, Founder of Modern Belgium.*

Ludwig, Charles. *Champion of Freedom.* Bethany House Publishers, 1987.

———. *He Freed Britain's Slaves.* Herald Press, 1977.

———. *Michael Faraday, Father of Electronics.* Herald Press, 1978.

Macalpine, Ida; and Hunter, Richard. *George III and the Mad Business,* 1969.

Marshall, Dorothy. *The Life and Times of Victoria.* Praeger, 1972.

Melville, Lewis. Vol. I and II. *An Injured Queen, Caroline of Brunswick.* Hutchinson & Co., 1912.

Middlemas, Keith. *Edward VII.* Doubleday, 1972.

Miller, Delia. *Queen Victoria in the Scottish Highlands.* Philip Wilson, 1985.

Nevill, Barry St. John. *Life at the Court of Queen Victoria, 1861–1901.* Webb & Bower.

Parker, John Stuart. *Sir Robert Peel.* John Murray, 1899.

Phillips, John A.S. *Prince Albert and the Victorian Age.* Cambridge University Press, 1981.

Phillips, Michael R. *George MacDonald, Scotland's Beloved Story Teller.* Bethany House Publishers, 1987.

Phillipson, D.W. *Mosi-oa-Tunya: A Handbook to Victoria Falls.* Longman, 1975.

Plowden, Alison. *The Young Victoria.* Weidenfeld and Nicholson, 1981.

Pollack, John. *Wilberforce.* Constable, 1977.

Pound, Reginald. *Albert, a Biography of the Prince Consort.* Simon and Schuster, 1973.

Railton, Herbert. *Westminster Abbey.* Macmillan, 1891.

Richardson, Joanna. *Victoria and Albert.* J.M. Dent & Sons, 1977.

Ridley, Jasper. *Henry VIII, the Politics of Tyranny.* Weidenfeld and Nicholson, 1984.

———. *Mary Tudor.* Weidenfeld and Nicolson, 1964.

Sanders, Edith. *The Hundred Days.* W.W. Norton, 1964.

Somerset, Anne. *William IV.* Weidenfeld and Nicholson, 1980.

Strachey, Lytton. *Queen Victoria.* Harcourt Brace & World, 1921.

Tim, Jeal. *Livingstone.* Putnam, 1973.

Trevelyan, G.M. *Lord Grey and the Reform Bill.* Longmans Green, 1920.

Tuchman, Barbara W. *A Distant Mirror.* Alfred Knopf, 1978.

Victoria, Queen. *Our Life in the Highlands.* The Folio Society, 1973.

Wheatcroft, Andrew. *The Tennyson Album.* Routledge & Kegan Paul, 1980.

Williams, Wells S. *The Middle Kingdom*, Vols. 1 & 2. A.H. Allen & Co., 1883.

Woodham-Smith, Cecil. *Queen Victoria*. Alfred Knopf, 1972.

Young, G.M. *Portrait of an Age*. Oxford University Press, 1936.